A VOYAGE to EXPLORE

A VOYAGE to EXPLORE

... Let's pay some heed to those silent whispers

Debarati Ray

EXCELLER BOOKS®
A GLOBAL PRESS

A Voyage to Explore
...Let`s pay some heed to those silent whispers

Cover by Exceller Books

ISBN: 978-93-47397-55-4

Published in India in 2025 by Exceller Books,
An imprint of GE Group,
G1, Dream Apartment, Degree College Road, Belgharia,
Kolkata, 700056, India
www.excellerbooks.com

EXCELLER BOOKS®
A GLOBAL PRESS

Dedicated to

My Father, Late Anath Kumar Ray

That powerful soul who not only helped me to make the decision to write this venture but also inspired me to gather up the broken pieces of my heart and show the world the real essence that I possess within. In his words, it would be like:

"Every single moment on this earth is nothing but a creation of God, and there is something beyond this mundane world, beyond this world of mundane reality, that I am not considering as the ideal world but something more powerful and with that magic to help us sustain in this tough world, and sometimes to make us feel that each of us has that magical potential within..."

My Mother, Shova Ray

That sweet and loving person who always helps me to remember my identity and always tries to be that polestar in the sky of my life. Her existence not only inspires me to explore my destination but also makes me feel that God is everywhere. In her words, I would like to say:

"Every work that we do on a regular basis in our daily life is nothing but a dedication to that supreme energy, controlling and protecting us with deep care and nourishment. And it is one of the parts and parcels of our life to be enlightened with the aura of that higher Truth more and more..."

Acknowledgements

On a superficial level of understanding, it would be utterly impossible for me to enlist the particular names of those persons to whom I wish to express my respect and gratitude. As I think, this gratitude and acknowledgement cannot be imprinted on a certain page or paper but must be nourished with love and affection of our heart and soul; these are to be remembered and preserved like a candle in a dark room.

A single note of appreciation would not be enough to justify the names or the circumstances that inspired me greatly to complete this venture. On a deeper level of comprehension, I would rather say that sometimes certain circumstances in our lives also teach us a lot in order to reach a point of fruitful exploration. In that sense, I would like to reinforce my point by sharing the fact that it is not always the people who inspire me all the time, but also some circumstances and events that sometimes help me to behold a mirror in front of myself and make me feel that I, too, have the same importance and existence as others.

In this connection, I would also like to acknowledge those events and incidents of my life that not only came to me as learning experiences but also helped me to know myself, inspired me to be what I am and what I would like to be. The meetings, the conversations, and the perceptions that I gained from those incidents sometimes revealed themselves as mere accidents, but at times they opened my eyes to the miraculous truths of life itself. Those meetings, those people, and the particular conversations with them gradually started to develop within me a different version of myself and helped me to unpeel the layers of those matters, ultimately leading me to unveil the ultimate truth lurking behind those superficial circumstances. Truly speaking, throughout the journey, those events somehow helped me to feel where lies the ultimate Truth itself, where lies the actual meaning of Life itself.

In each and every moment of this journey, I observe, penetrate, recognise, and ultimately come to a certain point of realisation, that is, from where I need to start my journey once again, or where I need to rest awhile, or exactly at which destination I need to anchor my ship.

As I reflect on myself some years back in this journey, I found nothing but darkness ahead. I was even totally unable to recognise my existence, but something happened in a miraculous way. All of a sudden, I started to feel a higher Truth of life itself that had no value, you may think, on a superficial level of understanding or from a material point of view, but it had a magical force within that allowed my heart and soul to perceive that infinite power of intelligence of the universe and ultimately led me to take up this project to be imprinted.

This is why, once again, I would like to remind you that enlisting only a few particular names and acknowledging them as the sole force behind this venture would not be wise enough; rather, there is a different story, a higher force that is always at work to protect and guide us all. I would like to acknowledge the higher force of intelligence that somehow helped me to write this project and guided me to feel that we all have a divine essence within and that we are nothing but spiritual beings in a mortal body.

Few Words to My Readers

Sometimes life seems to me like a paperback storybook. Sometimes it appears as a mirage. At other times, life is a mirror. In it, I not only see my reflection, but also glimpse my destiny. It makes me aware that I am on a voyage—on a voyage indeed...

A voyage to unfold, and to explore in an extraordinary way. You need not recognise how or why the incidents are gradually taking their place. Yet you may still be surprised by the consequences of the incidents the characters have faced. (For confidentiality, most character names, their professions, and locations have been changed.) Sometimes those incidents appeared in their lives as disguised blessings. Sometimes, they arrived as nightmares. And herein lies the power of their being, the power of their existence, the power of God's miracle!

In that sense, this book is a tribute to those enlightened souls. They not only helped me open my eyes but also taught me to see the tangible world in a different way. They also inspired me to believe in that supreme power of intelligence. They made me feel that each of us holds unique potential to explore this mundane world through a different lens.

Debarati Ray

Introduction

At first glance, or rather, in a superficial way of understanding, the title of this book may seem vague, as if it is about an ordinary voyage that ultimately leads you towards a hackneyed destination as always. But if you delve deeper into it, you may feel those silent whispers; you may perceive something beyond this mundane world of materialistic journeys and gradually begin to believe that here on this earth we are nothing but spiritual beings in human form. All of us may have our own purpose, a different voyage as well. Yet, in spite of that, quite miraculously we have all embarked on a voyage, not even knowing where the destination is, where we are going. But we are on a journey, longing for that higher truth. In a way, it may be considered that we are all here to know where lies our soul's choice, where lies the deeper meaning of our essence, where lies the sole purpose of our life.

Actually, I had no intention of writing this venture at first. It was neither a forced work nor a venture written according to any previous plan; it just came to me quite accidentally. It simply happened. In that sense, it is nothing but a fruitful exploration of a revelation I experienced a few years back. During those days, quite unexpectedly, life helped me to confront several incidents. I started to jot them down in a leisurely manner. But that task gradually became a spontaneous source of strength for me. Most days, I used to meet people from different professions, have conversations with them, and sometimes those conversations or events appeared before me as revelations of a different kind. Gradually, day by day, all those incidents ultimately led me to realise that here on this earth we actually have different purposes as our soul's choice. There is a higher force guiding and protecting us beyond this mundane world of reality, irrespective of our economic, cultural, or geographical background.

On a superficial level of understanding, we cannot perceive this deep thought; we cannot imagine that beyond this mundane world there is something higher and pure that exists not only to protect but also to guide us in a miraculous way, even when life seems like a dark dungeon from which escape is utterly impossible. In that sense, I feel this book may help you perceive where lies the truth of life itself and may transcend your essence towards that divine light. You may start to realise that descending into the darker phases of life is not indulging in depression, but rather finding the secret code of your being, adopting the pace of silence and in a deeper way, deconstructing the enigma you possess within. Truly speaking, this book came to me as a blessing from that higher force that not only encouraged me to deepen my faith but also allowed my soul to become the foster mother of my being.

On a serious note, I would like to share a fact with all of you. This book is actually a compendium of several of my blogs that have already been published on my website, *debaratiray.com*, where I regularly try to connect with my readers, writing on spiritual topics and sharing experiences that moved my heart and touched my soul in different ways. At first, I did not take this venture seriously. But gradually, people began to read my blogs, send their feedback and inspire me to take this project as a serious literary venture. I never paid much heed to their words; rather, I continued to gain more experiences and write them down regularly on my website.

Then something happened, all of a sudden. I started to realise that the blogs I was typing during those days were not written by me; they were appearing on the screen automatically, more spontaneously. For the first few days, I did not understand the process. But the more I became attached to it, the more I began to feel the magic, and quite miraculously I felt that it was not me doing the task, but some higher force continually guiding me forward and enlightening me with the truth of life itself.

It may sound quite baffling and may seem illogical to some of you, lacking any rationality. But herein lies the mystery of writing this book; herein lies the true essence of those silent whispers. Moreover, herein lies the history of this extraordinary voyage and the mystery of creating this literary venture. From a superficial point of view, this exploration may seem to you nothing more than the product of imaginative thought. But if you delve into it, you can feel that it is the eternal longing of our soul for which we have all been waiting since the primordial time of our existence.

Some of you may think that the incidents I am going to talk about are nothing but creative fantasies or spiritual imaginations that we sometimes indulge in during the mournful hours of our life. But if you probe deeper, you will feel that this is not a mere imagination to harp on but an experience to behold forever; an experience to feel the divinity within, an experience to balance ourselves and communicate with the contemporary world through love and compassion.

And herein lies the utility of this extraordinary yet spiritual experience. Herein lies the effectiveness of surrendering our being to that higher level of intelligence and feeling the magic in a divine way. In that sense, the more you go through this venture, the more you may start to feel that every page of this book is actually a tribute to that higher power of intelligence that is not merely visible to us but is and will always be, not only surrounding the universe but also within the core of our being.

Table of Contents

1 | Adopt the Pace of Silence and Feel Your Soul

"It was all in that silence, in that absolute silence of my depth, I got to know wherein lies my true power; the real worth of my existence. Somehow, I gained a different insight into a different world; a world beyond this tangibility, but the world of an eternal reality where I felt that I was in close communion with my deeper self, my silence within. She was trying to say something! Though inaudible at first, I felt that inner stillness was somehow guiding me to delve deeper within my entity to feel that silence more profoundly, in a way where I could explore only my inner kingdom and its eternal presence once again, its connection with the divinity that I already have within since the primordial time of my existence. It was truly a different experience for me and the moment I started to feel that solitude within, quite miraculously, all the distress and dissatisfaction I was suffering from started to fade away and in that absolute tranquillity, I perceived the real truth of my existence once again."

In this cacophonous world of survival, when at every moment time comes to us as a seizing monster, we get frightened, pause for a while and ask ourselves, with awe and wonder, where this life is trying to lead us. But at that very moment, I suggest you not to fall into the trap of those dissatisfactions. Rather, calm your mind and sit for a while, putting aside all momentary worries and concerns, and ask your inner self the same question you once posed. I can assure you that you will not be disheartened. It may invite you into another world of your existence, where you can perceive the efficacy of detaching from this clamorous outer world for a while and aligning with your inner self, who always chooses to speak to you and undeniably listens to you. Despite her absolute silence, you can still perceive wherein lies the true power of this close communion.

You remember, at the beginning of this chapter, I already shared with you one such experience of a woman who was totally devastated after a fatal incident in her life. She was utterly ruined in every respect, and she couldn't gather herself once again, being in this noisy world of continuous distractions and dissatisfactions, where all the time, you cannot find any other option but to accept those noisy negatives and act like a prisoner of your own negative thoughts.

But the moment she began to learn and feel the silence within, with the help of a psychoanalyst, she quite naturally began to be introduced to a different world of understanding; the world of her inner self, where silence was not silent at all. Rather, it was that silence within which brought back to her the clear answers she had long been seeking. It was only in the midst of that silence that she once again aligned with her ideal being, with the strength of her existence, and somehow, quite miraculously, managed to forget all her sorrows to emerge before the world with the truth she held, with the real power of her being.

Finding Silence within Is Nothing but Being Aligned with Your Inner Kingdom Once Again

In order to feel the true power of silence, you need to pay heed to Nature, which evolves at her silent pace. Yet she is growing within, leaving us only to witness her magical transformation. If we ask her wherein lies the secret, she will not say anything, but we can feel her answers deep within that profound silence, she maintains around us.

In this connection, I would like to remind you that finding silence is not only about detaching yourself from external worldly sounds while engaging your inner world with the same cacophony, ruminating over the same noisy negatives that can ultimately do nothing but stress you and make you feel that you are a hopeless prisoner trapped in turmoil, in those negatively noisy and dissatisfying thoughts. Here, I would like to speak of that inner silence that we all have within, but never allow ourselves to feel its magic in solitude. If we delve into that silence, we will never be disheartened again. Rather, we will be introduced to a different reality, the truth of our being, the real self of our existence. It is in that absolute silence alone that you will get aligned with your primordial centre and once again be introduced to the eternal ground of your being from where you came and into which you will merge.

The more you delve into that inner quietude, the more you'll get to know who you really are and what your true purpose is in this world of existence. In this connection, I would like to remind you that if we wish to perceive our soul once again, we must feel that silence within. We need to pay some heed to its ineffability, to its inexplicability. As it is in that silence, our soul has her eternal existence; she is nothing to be touched, nothing to be described in an analytical way of observations, but an eternal energy to be perceived within, within the stillness of our entity, within the silence of our heart.

Here, being in close communion with silence doesn't mean detaching yourself from the external hurly-burly. Rather, here silence means probing more within your depth, inside your soul's kingdom, where at first you may be overwhelmed, startled a bit, but with time you come to realise the true worth of detaching yourself from all those materialistic needs and noises of your surroundings and getting aligned with the deeper core of your being that never speaks in an audible way But answers come quite automatically when you yourself can feel that your entity is totally aligned with that profound silence within. And at that very moment, once again, you are introduced to the secret code of your being that continually beckons you to perceive the eternal stream of life, the stream of your inner silence, who only knows the truth of your existence, the truth of an eternal reality as well.

Moreover, this silence has an enormous effect on both the psychological and spiritual way of our being. It has the ability to evolve our consciousness towards a different direction in a self-reflective manner, where we ourselves are introduced to our true ground of being. And in this deeper state of silence, quite automatically, the doors of our perception start to open up by themselves, and an infinite abundance starts to flow within with the help of pure consciousness, and we get to know that we're not alone in this world, but rather very much connected to the eternal truth of universal intelligence (who is already within us, within that profound silence deep inside our entity and continually inspires us to know ourselves and evolve in a newer way, true to our soul's choice).

Let's Feel the Power of Silence and Get Introduced to the Transcendental Reality of Your Existence

Spending some hours alone, contemplating that silence within, not only helps open your doors of perception but also transcends your consciousness into a different state of realisation. In that blessed state, we're more attuned to the spiritual dimension of our existence, and our ordinary consciousness quite miraculously transcends itself into that special type of pure consciousness that quite automatically starts to inspire us to grow within, to feel our being once again, and to get ourselves introduced to our primordial existence.

This power of silence is enormous enough. It can see beyond, beyond this tangible world of earthly perceptions, beyond everything that seems ordinary to us. And herein lies its magic, its beauty of perceiving the truth within in a different way. And gradually, being in that silence, we start to feel grounded once again.

In that moment of inner quietude, you align quite automatically with the truth of our universal intelligence and your eternal connection to that energy once again. And no longer would this same frustrating life appear before you as a hopeless one, but rather as something blissful and peaceful enough, because by that time your soul is already aligned with the truth of your spiritual existence; an existence that is beyond this momentary timeframe, beyond this world of tangibility, but an existence that always advocates an eternal reality. And herein lies the blissful essence of our inner silence and its magical connection with our spiritual existence.

"When the external world frustrates you a lot
Never feel disheartened, my dear
Never feel the same again.
Rather, sit for a while
Close your eyes and ask yourself.
Is it going to be a newer ride?
You may not find any answer, my dear
Any graceful story for others to share
Noisy giants may come across,
Sometimes to mock at you, sometimes to shake your ground.
But never fall under his trap.
Rather, probe more within; there, you may feel an absolute serenity,
A complete peace to feel within, and here once again
You may perceive
A star is shining with all its primordial shine,
Primordial silence within,
With the truth of its eternal grace,
With the truth that you are and will be,
With all your presence…"

Let's Heal Your Wounds in Silence and Allow Your Creator Within to Emerge in a Newer Way

In this current generation of cybernetic facilities, we are constantly running after something, only to ultimately find nothing that may satisfy our hearts and souls. As a result of that, quite unknowingly, we are coming towards a state of incongruence, a state where we face a constant dilemma within but cannot find the real reason behind it. Here in this section, I would like to tell you the real cause of this incongruence that sometimes impels us to take unfavourable decisions and sometimes prompts us to feel that we are nothing but hopeless wanderers, strolling around here and there without any vital purpose. But the reality is not like that. It is only an illusion to consider ourselves lonely wanderers, while actually, we are not alone at all but eternally connected to a divine source of universal energy.

But do you ever feel where does that universal source of energy reside? How are we connected to it? In this section, I would like to invite you into that different dimension of our being, into that reality that we so often forget while spending time in this external world amidst its continuous cacophony. Every moment, we tend to forget the real power of our inner stillness, the power of silence that holds an eternal magic to explore our creative intelligence and strengthen our insight in a more positive way, bringing clarity and transcending our consciousness towards the greatest truth of existence. Though in a tangible sense, you may not see anything, the moment you start to probe deeper into the silence within, you will quite automatically realise where the truth lies—the eternal and universal power of silence and our connection to the divine source of universal intelligence.

Maintaining that silence actually has an enormous effect on your psychological and spiritual well-being. It not only calms your mind but also opens up the doors of perception in a fruitful way, strengthening your confidence, improving your intellectual power, and unfolding the hidden magic of your intellect. It makes you realise that you are not a hopeless wanderer but someone with potential and a special purpose on this earth, for which you are here, for which you are born. Here I am going to share with you some of the benefits of practising this silence within:

- In silence, you can achieve that state of mind where you can stand in front of a mirror to see yourself in a reflective way. And trust me, dear, this is not an ordinary reflection in a mere sense, but a reflection to see within—within your being—and spend some hours of solitude with your soul, who keeps waiting for you, never complains but only waits to listen to your sweet voice. You may be surprised a bit, but trust me, dear, herein lies the magic of silence!
- Only that inner silence has the power to communicate with your soul, with that primordial self of your being, and can heal your wounds through a deeper realisation within yourself. At this stage, you may realise who you truly are. It not only presents you with that ideal mirror to perceive yourself, but also helps you accept who you are in a more mature and profound way.
- In a fit of anxiety or stress, when the external layer of your conscious self is not in proper congruence with the deeper core of your inner self, trust me, dear, silence is the only way to perceive your inner experience in a more contemplative way. It has an enormous effect in bringing you back to your centre, to your home from where you came and to which you will return after this earthly existence.
- Silence has its own language, a language of empathy and understanding, through the grace of which you will be able to forgive others and yourself. Its serenity will help you realise the real truth behind everything. It brings that eternal feeling of peace within yourself and helps

you to ground yourself once again in the truth of your being. In a more exploratory sense, it has the enormous gift of communicating with your soul and making you believe that you also have an artist within, waiting for your assurance to emerge in its true self to paint a new picture according to your soul's choice, and to bring serenity to your heart.

- In simpler terms, silence can bring you into a state of being where, quite automatically, you start to accept yourself and to believe in your soul's power, eradicating all forms of egoistic bias and becoming willing to evolve in a newer way in a different direction. In a way, silence has that rejuvenating power to blur all your dilemmas and conflicts and to reveal before you another reality, another truthful dimension of your being, introducing you to the grace of that eternal, sublime peace from where you came and to which you will return.

Moreover, it helps you recognise the true creator within yourself, who not only knows your depths but also has the power to heal you once again from all the wounds you are suffering from, speaking to your depths and nourishing them in a newer way. It is not an overnight process to feel that silence within; it is an inner exploration, a psycho-spiritual journey to perceive its real power. And it is in this state of silence that creation comes in a spontaneous way, and quite naturally, you may start to feel the urge to emerge before the world completely anew, yet true to yourself.

Feeling the Silence Within Is Nothing but Gaining a Spiritual Insight and Feeling the Divinity and Bliss Once Again

A few years back, when I was in my early teens, I had an experience as well. Though in those days I didn't know wherein lay the true power of silence and its connection with spirituality. It was utterly impossible for me to define spirituality in those early years when most of the time my mind used to search for various candid experiences, and my heart used to run after different colours of joy and merrymaking. But in those days, whenever I stood under the starry sky at night, I used to feel something different, though incapable of knowing what that feeling really was all about.

Years later, gradually with time, I perceived that the starry sky of those silent nights was nothing but a mirror itself, making me feel that I was not alone at all. Rather, my inner stillness was very much aligned with the silence of those nights since the primordial time of my existence. And it was only these messages that those silent nights used to convey in those years. Though inaudible it might have been, it had a special language that is still now throbbing within me and inspiring me to surrender to that absolute silence once again, to that absolute serenity that is already within us in a transcendental way.

The moment you are introduced to that absolute silence you possess within, your ordinary consciousness starts to bloom in a newer way, in a different direction towards transcendental reality, helping you gain deeper spiritual insight and realise that you are nothing but a spiritual being in human form. Hence, your existence itself is both real and eternal; real in its very presence and eternal in its divine essence.

In that silent state of your mind, you will not only be able to perceive more beyond this tangible world of perceptions, but also quite naturally become aligned with your pure consciousness and start to realise that your soul is already connected to that eternal universal intelligence who is nurturing, guiding and sheltering your being in a miraculously blissful way.

If we consider our life a spiritual journey, I feel attaining silence is the only pathway to experiencing that journey in a fruitful and peaceful way. It not only helps you to be detached from the external environment and the continuous hurly-burly raising its voice in the form of discord and disequilibrium, but also guides you to feel another introspective journey that is going on within yourself. In that sense, silence is not merely to be felt when you are away from noise, restlessness, or other disturbances that may perturb your mind; this inner silence is actually to be perceived within. It has the ability to transcend your consciousness into a deeper realisation and evolve your soul towards a new direction, towards the truth of the infinite, towards the truth of your inner divinity and its eternal connection to the truth of our universal intelligence.

Remember, the more you align yourself with your inner silence, the more you will come to know the truth — the eternal reality of your being, the reality of your soul. And the moment you are introduced to this eternal truth, the magic of bliss quite automatically starts to embrace your being, and once again, you come to know wherein lies the true celebration of life, the real magic of this introspective journey, and the graceful essence of this silence since the primordial time of your existence.

If you delve into this silence, you may also find someone's sweet voice still humming within, making you feel that you are not alone but deeply connected to an enigmatic force within, to that voice of eternity whose only language is not to be interpreted but to be perceived within, in the deeper core of your being:

Beyond this city crowd,
Beyond this cacophony, where the earth
Still meets with the clouds –
Only there, you can feel me, my dear,
Only there, you find my presence,
My story to share.
Only in that absolute silence,
Deep and rare!
You may find a reality;
A reality within,
That still knows
Wherein lies the truth,

The truth of eternity –
The truth that's still humming,
Growing within,
This time, perhaps,
A magical lore –
Quiet and serene!

2 | Find Out the Inner Truth: Feel Your Being

Only a cursory glance at the title may make you feel baffled. You may think, what is this inner truth I'm talking about, and what is its connection to making you feel in a different way? And most importantly, where does it reside? Sometimes you may feel that it comes quite spontaneously from yourself. But, on the other hand, you may even be puzzled to think what you actually are. Is it the ego? Or something that is far more different? Or is it that innermost depth of our entity where the psyche resides? But here, at this juncture, I would rather tell you that this Truth is a mysterious creative force that appears as a polestar, sometimes as a dove bringing peace and symmetry, sometimes as the phoenix to lift you up from the ashes of distractions and discomforts, and sometimes it also appears as the deep-down depth of an ocean to fill your entity with solace and serenity. You just need to feel it with all your spontaneity, with an inner grace that you already have within.

An Inspiration That Came in a Magical Way

Before I unravel this wonderful mystery, I would like to share a few excerpts from a short poem that came to me last night, out of the blue, in a drowsy state of my mind just before sleep. That was a mysterious creative force, somehow I felt beyond this world of tangibility, yet very much akin to my being, continually guiding me to mumble these words:

I am not an enigma, but your inner seed
Your soul to talk with
Here I am and will be forever.
Maybe a secret story to share.

You may be a bit surprised. But my explanation would be, herein lies the magic of seeing the world in a different way, where reality takes a magical turn with a subtle touch of transcendence, and your consciousness helps you to see the world with a different gaze, where transcendence and reality once again tie their knots and rename themselves as the transcendental reality.

A Happy Abode of This Inner Truth: Layers of Your Mind

If you really want to know how that creative spark came to me that night, you have to peep into that inner land where our mind resides. So, dear, let's go for a ride and see how it really works in a surprising way!

Three Layers of Our Mind

- **External Mind:** This is the external layer of our mind that may be termed as an exterior-coated form of your conscious self that receives data from all external happenings, helping you to be aware of them and to use your intellect in a calculative and strategic way in order to make any decision. It is actually the repository of your conscious awareness and your conscious doings. Technically, it may be termed as the RAM of your mind. It collects every memory that you visualise from the outer world and stores them within the internal layer of your mind for further use. Sometimes it may also perform this process without your awareness. This layer is also connected to your Internal Mind.
- **Internal Mind:** This is the inner layer of your mind. It may be termed as the interior part of yourself. Usually, it

works as a two-way traffic system. Sometimes it channelizes its energy towards the external part of yourself, and sometimes it sends its signals towards your Inner Mind, the core part of your existence, which I will discuss later. It channelizes its signals with the help of three energies of yourself that are subtly linked to this layer.

The first energy is your **Survival Self**, which works with two undercurrents. The first is the **Normal Undercurrent**, which helps you to live according to the norms of your survival existence that keep you alive. The second is the **Undercurrent of your Ego**, which works both in good and bad ways. When it works in a self-centred manner, indulging a thought of self-absorption, that is, some sort of extra pride that everything can be done by you and you alone, and there is no other force around the universe required for anything else, then you have to think for a while, as here the ego may work in a negative way, keeping you completely unaware of its reverse effect. Sometimes it also works in a way that seems acceptable, devoid of any sense of self-absorption or self-gratification, yet it helps your conscious self to make vital decisions while keeping your self-esteem intact. In this case, it works for a better result and influences you to be more passionate and constructive, pushing you forward to find your true worth.

The second energy is your **Overwhelming Self**, sometimes influenced by social scenarios and sometimes by past life issues submerged and suppressed in your subconscious, resulting in anxiety, depression, irritations, fears and over-expectations when seeing the external world or experiencing emotional upheavals. Sometimes you may get overwhelmed by sudden incidental joy or sorrow. Whenever you get attached to these emotions, your energy is automatically channelized towards your external self, resulting in behavioural problems and other mental and physical issues. Consequently, you may lose your internal balance and, for a time, even your external balance.

The third energy is the **Intermediary Self**, clinging like a pendulum between these two energies. It is the state of your mind where all the conflicts and dilemmas arise, sometimes making you satisfied and sometimes leaving you dissatisfied. As a result, you may lose your confidence. In this state, you may feel very energetic, but as it moves towards your *Overwhelming Self*, you may feel disturbed, resulting in a conflict in your normal thought process that immediately influences the conscious layer of your mind and all other aspects of your everyday life.

- **Inner Mind:** This is the innermost depth of your Internal Mind, the inner core of your being. This state of mind cannot be reached through the conscious realisation of your tangible reality, but it has its presence in an unseen world of reality that has existed since your beginning. It is invisible but has a deeper connection to your being. It cannot be seen, interpreted with rationality, or defined in an etymological form of theoretical analysis. It is spontaneous and independent, and its infinite wisdom and creative intelligence can only be felt through a deeper knowing of yourself.

When you breathe, you may think it is your conscious self that is helping you to do so, but I would rather suggest that it is not only the external part but also an inner mystery, your life force itself, helping you to breathe and feel, always inviting you towards that unseen world of vitality and rejuvenation. Herein lies the happy abode of your Inner Truth, your true companion, your Soul. Whenever you seek some recluse to spend time with yourself, you may feel the secret and soft mumblings of your soul. It may come in the form of an epiphany, intuition or deeper feeling. It may also emerge as poetic expression (as it did in my case) or as some soulful music that unexpectedly touches your heart within a moment and welcomes you into a different realm of consciousness — a consciousness beyond any logical interpretation, beyond any tangible sense of rational comprehension.

However, in this connection, I would like to tell you about another mysterious force that pervades our universe — the ultimate source of energy, a wonderful, all-pervading energy to which your Higher Self is connected with an eternal bond. This ultimate divine energy always guides and protects your soul for a higher purpose, a purpose you are destined for.

How Did a Miracle Happen to an Entrepreneur?

You'll definitely be awe-inspired if you listen to this incident that I'm going to share with you here. I've heard it from one of my friends who was a psychoanalyst by profession and who, quite unexpectedly, met someone who had once been a successful entrepreneur but, during those days when they met, had completely lost his faith to survive any longer. As a result, a sense of hopelessness made him mumble these words: "I only need something that may lead me to my next lifetime."

When asked by my friend, "But you're still surviving. So what do you think about this lifetime?" his answer was, "This is only the messy one. I don't want to survive any longer."

In his real life, an unfortunate disaster had actually happened to him. He had lost his business, his family, and the prosperous life he had once enjoyed. All other ties and pleasures of this tangible world that normally make someone content to survive had been literally wiped out of his life. Then, only a few of his friends felt that he needed some consultations to get himself back on his feet.

In this connection, I would like to tell you that my friend used to treat his patients very kindly, and, naturally, this was no exception. On their first meeting, he asked, "So, how are you going, man?"

After hearing that, the man looked perplexed and answered in a stern way, "I'm not here to have this discussion. I need your help, and this is not a joke. I'm going through a crisis." He finished that line with a stern look.

"But I see you're absolutely perfect," my friend replied, but that made him more furious, and he started to scream, "I don't want to survive any longer! Do you have that special thing that'll lead me to my next lifetime?"

"But why, my dear?" my friend asked him politely.

"Because it's utterly a hellish experience for me to survive any longer," he replied in a dejected mood.

"Yes! I, too, feel the same way. Would you give me your postal address?" my friend asked.

"But why?" the man asked, annoyed a bit.

"So that I can send that special thing to you. But please keep in mind that you'll have to share all your secret plans with this special thing every morning—the things you wish to have in your next lifetime. Plan them, nurture them, and believe in your heart that you're receiving them right now. If possible, do this three times a day; you'll surely make it happen," my friend replied.

"Will it work?" he asked.

"Absolutely! That'll be a magical crystal," my friend assured him, bringing a habitual smile to his face.

Six months later, an envelope was posted to my friend's address. There was a letter inside:

> *"Hi! Dear,*
> *I want to return that crystal you gifted me because now I have it within me, and my inner crystal continually helps me to learn not to leave this world, but to live, believe, and live once again!"*

When Psyche Meets Her Mate, Miracle Is the Only Consequence

Are you surprised? Let me explain in a more explorative way. An utter failure in his life and the related depression had totally made that entrepreneur helpless. All these upheavals and negative thoughts quite unconsciously started to reach towards the Overwhelming Self of his mind. At the same time, his ego self couldn't accept that failure any longer and continually tried to push him forward. But in his conscious mind, he was unable to find anything significant to make his life as it had been before.

Here, his survival self became perturbed again and started to betray itself. And at this point, conflicts and dilemmas within his intermediary self began to channelize their energy directly into his external conscious mind, resulting in hopelessness, behavioural problems, and an utter reluctance to survive any longer.

But there's a mystery in it. Hope you already got my point. Like you all, he also had a true mate, his soul, connected to the divine source of energy. This force continually directed his energy towards an unseen world of reality where truth resides, and it was because of this force that he used to talk about his next lifetime in an unexpected way. The psychologist readily understood that point and used that crystal only as a symbol, as an external stimulus to rejuvenate his soul once again, who had lost her way in the midst of his surviving ego self and overwhelming self, and felt herself badly stuck in that intermediary self, yet struggling at the same time to be in her own essence, to be in her own accord.

After sharing his plans with that crystal, that entrepreneur not only released his negative thought patterns but also began imprinting useful thoughts into his mind. At the same time, he was introduced to the highest truth, very much aligned with the core of his existence. Do you want to know where did he get that support? Absolutely, it was all from his Inner Mind, his divine self, whose tendency was always to make him feel complete and content within, with all his higher potentials, and to help him realise his eternal connection to that ultimate source of divine energy.

As it happened, his external conscious self automatically received that positive undercurrent and in the meantime the disequilibrium he was experiencing found a constructive balance, resulting in a miracle with the blink of an eye. This divine magic not only healed and nurtured his soul but also recreated him in a newer way, allowing him to believe in an unseen world of reality where truth exists in an eternal and invincible way.

In this connection, I would like to suggest that if you are unable to find your inner truth, just start preparing your higher self to connect to the divine source of energy and see the magic within. I can assure you, there you can never find any upheaval or conflict lurking between your overwhelming and intermediary selves. Your ego (in a good sense) can also channelize its energy in a fruitful way, and you may start to feel that a mysterious, creative force is leading you towards a state of bliss in a constructive way. Then only you can explore the true state of your being and comprehend the true purpose of your existence on this plane, not as a barren existence but as a gift from the universe.

A Sweet Reminder to Feel and Evolve Your Being in a Peaceful Way

Self-reflection, a kind of inner knowing, is highly needed as it helps you connect to your higher self, your true soulmate that's intrinsically linked to the eternal divine energy, the ultimate life force of your existence. Now I'm going to share with you the secret of how to feel that eternity within yourself and how to restore it as a continuous power centre of your being. Through recognising this truth, you may automatically gain a sense of integrity within your being and a need to evolve yourself with a consciousness of higher knowing.

Preferably, during the time of dawn, you can maintain this method. If not, then try to do it at least once a day at a suitable time when you feel free and relaxed from the external world.

- First, relax your body, breathe in and out naturally while sitting in a comfortable position.
- Then try to calm your mind, but don't pressurise yourself to do so; let it happen naturally.
- You may feel all the distractions coming haphazardly into your mind. Don't get bewildered. It's natural, as we are all human beings and we have a precious mind to think over.
- Try to imagine yourself sitting on a sea beach during sunrise. Feel that wonder of nature. Feel that you're blessed enough to experience that eternal beauty within.
- Imaginatively, you may visualise the waves flowing on the surface of the sea. You may also hear the sounds of those waves. Remember, those waves are nothing but the upheavals of your life continually hitting the shore of your conscious self and sometimes over the intermediary part of your inner self, causing conflicts again.
- Try not to indulge yourself in those thoughts. Instead, feel the calmness and serenity that prevail deep within the sea. Breathe in gently. Try to feel that you're not alone; rather, the entire universe is with you, and your whole being is getting aligned to that. Contemplate that you have peace and harmony within yourself. Try to feel that, despite those waves on the external surface, the sea itself remains calm within, and this is why it never misses the opportunity to see the sunrise at every dawn.
- Try to have those feelings within yourself. This serenity will automatically help you to feel your divine self. Gradually, you may hear what your inner guidance is trying to tell you — perhaps some precious

interpretations you never found before, a newer truth of your existence.

By applying this method, you may feel the ideal contentment your soul has been longing for and may start to realise your soul's purpose, which you have been destined for since your primordial existence. Moreover, with her subtle, intuitive assurance, you may never feel your life as a fruitless existence but treasure it as an oasis where the flowers need not have others' attention to bloom, yet always feel blessed within with the fragrance they already possess, since eternity.

3 | Let's Breathe and Feel Your Divine Essence Within

Though in an etymological sense 'to breathe' is nothing but only a physiological process where air moves in and out of our body through our nostrils and we feel relaxed and satisfied, bringing that effectiveness to our body, actually it is something more than that; an integral force that is essential not only for our sustenance or living but also for our life itself in the truest sense. Apparently, it is an absolutely normal physiological process through which we all undergo spontaneously, remaining unaware that breathing is closely associated with the truth of our aliveness. Yes! Herein lies the magic, the efficacy to feel the essence of your being, the essence of your entity!

And the moment you start to feel that grace within, quite automatically you begin to perceive that this breathing is a gateway leading your consciousness towards a deeper dimension, allowing you to perceive the inner space within your entity. This conscious breathing not only helps you be with your presence but also enables you to transform yourself through the higher truth of your soul. In that very moment, quite automatically, you may start to feel that this breathing is not only in close communion with your mundane body but also aligned with the grace of that highest truth from where you came into this existence; that magical presence of your inner self which is nothing but the insubstantial, divine part of your being, that inevitable life force continually strengthening your existence with the help of that universal divine intelligence since eternity.

So, this conscious breathing not only helps you recognise the inner space within your entity but also serves as a mediating force between your conscious and unconscious selves, reminding you of the highest truth of your life: the truth that you are alive with all your presence and all your grace within.

Let's Breathe and Explore That Inner Space You've Within

It was neither a trance-like state,
Nor an oblivion where I lost myself...
But a journey indeed, I felt;
A journey to feel my presence;
A meditation to feel that inner grace!

It was absolutely one of my personal experiences that quite spontaneously, came to this poetic fruition. It was not only a poem, but a self-reflective journey through which we all undergo, yet never care to feel that bliss within. Yes! This poem was only a slice of that blissful journey that I felt at that special moment when I was breathing. At that moment, I also perceived that I was not only alive with my very presence but also very much aligned with the truth of that higher grace that is always leading our energy towards that higher dimension of everlasting bliss, where our own spirit is already connected to that divine source of intelligence from which we all have come into this existence.

At that very moment, I was neither conscious nor unconscious but very much alert, very much in that present moment with all my presence and all my aliveness. Here I am not discussing the mundane existence that we all have, but here in this chapter I am trying to navigate into the deeper core of our existence that is subtly connected to this breathing experience.

In this connection, I would like to remind you that breathing is neither an act that we all do nor a form or material that we can see or touch. Instead, it is something that happens in a spontaneous, independent way, and we can only feel or experience it as a mere experiencer. It cannot be defined in a traditional way; herein lies the true meaning of our existence and its connection to this source of breathing. But one thing must be admitted: we all have a deeper existence beyond this mundane one, and this breathing is nothing but a mediatory force to discover that inner space in a deeper way, transporting our consciousness towards that higher dimension of eternity and enabling us to feel our presence in an uninterrupted, spontaneous way.

Being aware of your presence, that you are alive with all your hidden grace inside, is nothing but the ideal way to get back to your centre within. And that is why, in order to recognise that inner space, you need to be grounded once again. Once again, you need to be aligned with the divine source of universal intelligence, the centre of your origin, from where you came.

In order to be centred in your being and to feel that you are alive, you need to recognise that insubstantial inner space within your entity. That inner space does not have any form or appearance in a tangible sense, but it is that consciousness itself which may enable you to feel that you are alive inside; that blissful aliveness where your entity is closely aligned with the divine source of universal intelligence. And at that very moment, quite unknowingly, you may perceive that you are beyond your mundane body or your human existence, yet you are very much present within yourself. You are very much aligned with your inner essence, with the stillness you have within, since eternity. The more you connect to that stillness inside, the more you become aligned with the truth of that higher dimension within your own entity that is ageless, timeless and formless. And the moment you become aligned with that stillness within, quite automatically, you may start to feel that your consciousness is leading you towards a higher dimension beyond this mundane form of earthly existence. And there you have nothing but that consciousness, blissful and eternal. Herein lies the efficacy of breathing, and herein lies its magic to lead your consciousness towards the recognition of that inner space where we are all integrally aligned with the essence of our presence since eternity.

You're Not Lost but You're with Your Very Presence

At first, you may feel that you're losing yourself. But actually, you're not losing yourself; rather, you are gradually getting aligned with the universal source of divine intelligence, and your entity is merging with that very aliveness that is the intrinsic part of your being. The more you start to breathe, the more you may get aligned with the divine within your entity, and quite automatically, all the gaps and inconsistencies start to fade away in the blink of an eye. Quite unknowingly, you may discover that you're awakening to the truth of your being.

Once you awaken to the truth of that higher grace throbbing within your entity, enlightenment will not only come to embrace you, but at the same time, you will be introduced to the truth of your very presence. The moment you awaken to the truth of your very presence, quite unknowingly, you will be in alignment with your true purpose, the purpose that is deeply connected to your being, to your very presence, to the consciousness that is ageless and eternal.

And trust me, herein lies the grace of your presence, the grace of your inner space, the grace of that true alignment with the divine essence that is already in harmony with your entity in an inconspicuous yet magical way.

Let's Breathe and Feel Your Eternal Grace Within Yourself

In this contemporary world, where we are constantly suffering from anxiety, stress, and disorder, breathing not only helps our body to be relieved, but also helps our mind and heart to release all those stresses, leading our consciousness to that higher dimension from where life may not seem to us a fruitless survival lingering on gibberish and futility. Rather, it may appear as a blessing in itself, as something truly aligned with our very presence, the true aliveness of our being.

The deeper dimension of your being can only be perceived when you become aligned with that centre within your entity. Breathing does nothing but help you return to that centre once again, enabling your inner seed to flourish anew with the highest truth of aliveness itself. And herein lies the depth of your existence, the depth of your being.

Yes, herein lies the mystery of life itself, the mystery of our soul and her eternal connection to the universal power of divine intelligence. During the period of conscious breathing, our souls are not only open to the highest dimension but are also deeply aligned with the highest truth of our existence, the highest truth of that universal intelligence from where we all came into this earthly existence.

If you just close your eyes and breathe, allowing the flow to be spontaneous, quite automatically, you may start to experience your very presence. It's an exploration, indeed, a self-reflection to recognise that inner space—a gateway to finding balance between your mundane and divine selves. In that sense, this breathing acts as a stimulus not only to heal you from all the stresses and anxieties you suffer in your waking life, but also to enliven your soul with the highest truth of your presence, transcending your consciousness into the grace of the Infinite.

Only then, quite miraculously, you may start to feel that all the doors of perception are cleansed, and your entity is becoming more and more aligned with the highest truth of your existence. And that highest truth of existence is nothing but the consciousness itself — ageless and eternal — the consciousness that is divinely guided and the supreme principle behind everything. It has no form or matter, no birth or death in any tangible sense. It has existed since the eternal time of your being and will continue even after the death of your mundane body.

It is exactly this awakening that the process of breathing helps you to experience, helping you to perceive who you truly are beyond your ego, beyond your mundane form and identity, your divine essence and its eternal connection to the universal truth of divine intelligence.

4 | Let's Tune with the Rhythm of Nature: Transform and Grow Within

Deep into the woods as I stepped inside
I didn't know why, but I felt I needed to hide
From all the cacophonies drumming outside, heralding their presence,
Harking me back to enjoy another graceful ride.
Yes! They're introducing themselves...
Screaming aloud, "Yes! We're that civilisation instead!"
But I startled for once; didn't feel like going back, all at once.
Rather, I felt like shedding off my shell altogether,
Just to find a beauty within,
Just to have a sip, a sip of that eternal stream,
Flowing within the woods, keeping us unknown,
That, like her, we too have an eternal home,
Beyond this hustle and bustle, beyond every morning,
When civilisation knocks at our door,
Beyond this heraldic presence,
Where still we wander around, around some fruitless hopes.
Yes! We too have that eternal home,
That still invites us to harp on a sweet lore,
To feel the idyllic beauty,
Where twilight still descends over the blue hills,
And the dark pine forests still know
How to grow within.

You may think for a while, may be curious sometimes, what made me startle at once when the heraldic civilisation was harking me back, but I chose to hide myself in the lap of nature. In this connection, in order to satisfy your curiosity and to solve the mystery that makes you feel I'm only an introvert who likes to keep herself hidden from the advancing civilisation, I would like to tell you that the truth is not like that. Rather, it was all because of a hidden secret of our entity that we all possess within, quite unknowingly of ourselves. And that secret is nothing but our eternal connection to nature, to our mother earth, who always inspires us to transform and grow within.

But here, 'transformation' doesn't mean forgetting our roots and getting caught up in numerous distracting activities, thinking we're up to date enough to access any kind of facilities in this modern civilisation. Rather, here 'transformation' means to evolve ourselves once again, following the secret whispers of our soul, which is inextricably connected to nature, to our eternal life force.

Though I'm not saying that updating ourselves according to the parameters of this advancing civilisation is wrong, nor that we must be surrounded by sylvan forests where our only option is to lead a primitive life, I'm not suggesting that at all, as it may not be applicable for everyone. But here, I would like to remind you a simple fact.

And that fact is: how far we move away from our roots, however luxurious life we choose, however much this materialistic world pulls us back to the gloss and glitter of an extravagant lifestyle, ultimately, at the end of the day, we are all humans—very much natural, made of air, water, and soil. We are very much of the ground. We are the offspring of this Mother Earth. We also have our roots. We are here on this planet only to spread out our branches in a fruitful direction and to evolve our soul towards that path where eternity alone knows the secret—that our longing for nature is nothing but the longing of our inner seed to be in close communion with the divine, with that great artist of this entire creation.

Here, in this chapter, I would like to invite you into a different realisation where, quite naturally, you may start to feel that we're not a single entity, but very much connected to that universal source of energy. And at the same time, you may also become aware that, in the wilderness of nature, you may lose yourself for a while—not to hide from this external world as an introvert, but as a nature lover, as a seeker (and a believer in depth), in order to explore that mystery (that also made me hide that afternoon), wherein lies the truth of your real existence.

Let's Pay Some Heed to the Mountain Streams and Feel the Beauty Within

That afternoon is still distinct in my memory. It was a dusky one. The sun was preparing to rest after a long, tiring day. I was trailing along the meandering tracks of that solitary hilly region of Chamba, only to be a witness to that mesmerising beauty. My poetic soul was trying to mumble something, indistinct, I felt, but something about a deeper relationship! Yes, about a special connection, perhaps a faded one, I guessed.

The mists were swirling around the valley, descending down, perhaps trying to permeate their presence, wandering around and helping me to feel that I was not alone, but that wilderness had some message, some special mirror to behold. And I didn't know how, but something happened. Yes, magical it was! And somehow, I started to feel that the nature I was observing was not something external, but something very much aligned with my entity, with that eternal essence that I had been bearing within since the primordial time of my existence. I felt the beauty within. And somehow, in that solitude, all of a sudden, I started to feel that time paused for a while, only to behold that eternal gaze.

You may think it was only a mystical experience that I had. But trust me, dear, there was something magical that kindled in me a different realisation. That realisation didn't make me hold my photographic lens and capture the beauty in a technical frame. Rather, it made me rest for a while, hold a different mirror before myself, not only to feel the beauty within but to feel the language that nature speaks. And that language is of mutual sharing, of a divine love, of perceiving something higher beyond this tangible world, and of knowing the truth that nature still awaits those who love to speak with her, who love to know wherein lies the secret of their souls.

That dusky afternoon was nothing, but somehow it appeared before me as a mirror of realising something higher. And that poem (which I wrote that night, after returning to my hotel room) was nothing but a fruitful consequence of that realisation, where hiding myself for some time from this civilisation was not stupidity but an attempt to feel the serenity within and to allow my soul once again to reveal herself in her own way, to evolve and grow within, following those footsteps where the dark, dense forest still knows wherein lies the meaning of eternity itself.

Nowadays, most of the time, in the name of progress and technological evolution, we are advancing ourselves, sometimes even forgetting where the deeper core of our existence lies. We keep ourselves busy developing our civilisation while, quite unknowingly, neglecting our Mother Nature. And I think this is the consequence of feeling this lack within. Somehow, we start to feel that we are not complete enough. And once again, we fall into the trap of elusive thoughts that we think we can fulfil by seeking prosperity in the external world, completely ignoring the truth that we are already complete within.

So what we need to do is only to look within, to feel that eternal magic. And herein lies the significance of pausing for a while under the greener shades of a dense forest, resting your feet there for a while and discovering a newer version of yourself, very much aligned with the beauty of those forests, wandering through their secret passageways in the silence of those woods.

You may think, wherein lies the difference, or what would you gain simply by wandering around the woods, while our progressive civilisation keeps pushing us forward to enjoy the facilities of this advanced lifestyle in order to drink life to the lees? But here, at this juncture, I would like to remind you that this is the biggest mistake we usually make. Most of the time, we tend to view nature as something external, while actually, it is not like that. Rather, she is someone very much connected to our entity, very much akin to our being. And we are very much of her.

But in these contemporaneous scenarios, technological invasions have changed our perspectives. Day by day, we are becoming technology-oriented and, quite unknowingly of ourselves, forgetting our roots, our Mother Earth, the greater womb from which we came and will be merged into. Here I am not criticising technological prosperity, as technologies are also important for survival but in the name of technological progression, the more we estrange ourselves from nature, the more we sabotage our inner selves and at the same time deprive our souls' yearning to be connected to the divine.

For it is not nature who seeks healing through our communion, but we who need that healing from her. She is the eternal and perennial source of our being, our life force. But if we view her as something external, we may not feel wherein lies her ideal essence. Yet if we pause for a while beneath the starry sky at night, she will surely reveal her secret passageways. And at that very moment, you may start to feel that your consciousness is no longer functioning as a mere objective consciousness as before, but allowing you to transcend beyond this tangible world in order to feel the beauty and truth surrounding the entire universe.

And I must say, you may realise that the truth is of close communion, a truth of interconnectedness with the universal source of energy that is responsible for this entire creation, and that may help you to release your ego and make you feel who you truly are — the unexplored mystery of your existence, your aliveness as a whole. And quite naturally, you come to know that your existence has no end, as it had no beginning. Your presence is eternal and everywhere. And herein lies the beauty, the eternal truth of our existence that nature holds before us as a mirror.

Losing Yourself in the Lap of Nature Is Evolving Your Soul, Once Again

Losing yourself in the lap of nature is nothing but exploring yourself once again, true to your essence, to that primordial identity that is present within yourself every now and then. The more you estrange yourself from nature, the more you alienate your inner self from that real core of your existence.

You will never be able to feel where the true essence of nature lies unless and until you start to contemplate her and communicate with her in a spontaneous way. A true communion with nature is not like a cliché textbook reading and grasping some newer knowledge about ecological awareness, but rather something to be in close communion with nature, where you can be truly aligned with her beauty, not only to know the secrets that she always permeates, but the secrets of your divine existence and also of your special connection with this universe, since eternity.

In a way, communion with nature can be considered as a communion with the divine, where she holds before you that magic mirror in order to rediscover your inner self. And then you may start to feel that the murmuring streams of those misty, hilly regions may not appear before you as something external to see, but something very close to your being. The dense pine forests may not seem to you like some place unknown or distant; rather, that darkness may inspire you once again to free yourself from all the boundaries with which civilisation has shackled you in the name of progression. At the same time, it may help you to open your soul to the perfect silence of the woods, to a deeper realisation where even the darkness of the night has some special meaning to perceive.

In this connection, I would like to tell you that rationalisation of thoughts and envisioning nature as something external is the only barrier to feeling that bliss within. A deep, intense communion with nature will never leave you astray or make you feel that you are alone in this world, but rather help you to rediscover your being, which is very much aligned with her, in order to restore the beauty and the depth that you have within since the primordial time of existence.

That was an hour when the moonlit night started to speak to me; the mountain breeze was blowing in its own way, and I was gazing at the sky. The silence of that night had some beauty within, I felt, and that beauty was of eternity itself. There was something magical in it that made me realise that I am not apart from this world, but very close to this nature, to this art of creation. Standing beneath the starry sky of that night, a realisation suddenly stirred within me, and I became conscious of the reality that I am not a single entity, but I have a presence in eternity.

That night came to me as a state of revelation, and somehow I felt that it had been waiting for me for a long period of time only to share a mystery—the mystery of my existence, perhaps, the mystery of my soul, the mystery that still awaits for that moonlit night, for a different mirror to hold.

It was one of the experiences I had during my last visit to Chamba. The wilderness of that place not only overwhelmed me but also made me realise a deeper understanding. At that very moment, the calmness of the night and the twinkling stars did not appear before me as something external, but something very close to my heart. And herein lies the longing of our soul to be in communion with nature.

Being in nature does not mean viewing the scenic beauty and capturing it through some photographic lens; rather, to be in her company is to transcend our consciousness and open up our soul to feel the divinity that we have within. This close connection with nature may lead our consciousness to that level from which we can recognise who we truly are and what our connection is to this world of existence. We become more attuned to the true rhythm of our life, to that eternal tune of our existence that always inspires us to move forward, to transform and grow within, yet never allow ourselves to feel that we are leaving behind our roots forever (somewhat like the trees of those dense woods that transform and grow within, yet never leave their roots behind).

And herein lies the true meaning of our existence; herein lies our soul's heritage. It always helps us feel our being more spontaneously, in a way where our soul's language is the only one to be contemplated and perceived from the deeper core of reality itself. This is the change of consciousness that we may feel in direct communion with nature. Compassion may start to flow in its natural way, and humanity may once again colour its harmonious presence.

In a way, communion with nature not only helps us balance ourselves and maintain our psychological health, but it also nurtures our inner seed and makes us realise that we are not human machines, but spiritual beings in human form. Simply put, our soul is transformative in her essence, quite like nature itself—free to evolve and grow within, yet at the same time grounded by her roots. A close contact with nature always acts as a rejuvenating force, enabling us to regain our strength—the power we may have lost amid materialistic needs and technological invasions.

Here, 'transformation' does not mean changing yourself entirely and presenting yourself before the world as someone you are not; rather, it has a deeper meaning to be perceived. It means knowing your inner experiences in a more spontaneous way. And this is possible through a deeper communion with nature, where your soul has the freedom to spread its wings like wild geese and evolve in an unrestrained way. Once again, you may feel that you have nothing to do but to be with your real self in the midst of nature, with your eyes filled with awe and wonder, feeling who your true creator is. You may also realise that the creator is not someone from the external world, but someone within yourself.

In a deeper sense, this communion with nature is nothing but a soulful way to connect with the divine, to rekindle that eternal connection which we may have forgotten in the daily course of material needs and existential upheavals.

Do you know why most of us so often feel a longing for nature? I think that longing is not only for our Mother Earth but also for that eternal connection we share with the universal source of energy. And here, nature is nothing but a blessing sent from the universe, not only for our survival but to make us realise that following her path is the only way to feel our divinity within. In close communion with her, you may once again feel the grace of eternity within. And herein comes our true emergence—emerging before the world with our true, natural essence and evolving once again, while staying grounded with our inner seed.

Let's Align Yourself with Nature and Explore the Truth of Eternity

In this section, I would like to introduce you to a mystery, the eternal truth of our existence that most of the time we tend to ignore, yet at the same time feel a lack within. Actually, this lack is nothing but the yearning of our soul to be reconnected with her eternal home. And the only path to that home may be restored, I think, through a close communion with nature. This close communion can make us feel that we are not apart from this art of creation, from those blue hills, from the sunrise, or from that mountain stream that is still flowing in her own way, since the time we had not been on this earth in our mortal existence. But we had been in an eternal existence; yes, eternal it is, and herein lies the truth and beauty of our being, the harmony and reality of our existence.

Communion with nature not only heals your mind and body, but it also allows your soul to transcend beyond this tangible realm of understanding, introducing before you an alternative form of knowing yourself where depth can only speak with depth, and there you can find an inner you who will never lead you astray. Do you want to know why this happens? Because we have a close connection to nature, even when we do not have any earthly existence on this planet. When no one cares who you are, even when you yourself forget about your true identity, this Mother Earth will always remind you of your true worth. She will caress your wounds and embrace you once again, only to make you feel that you are and will be beyond this tangible realm of consciousness, beyond this earthly existence. So, separation from her is nothing but an illusion, as we are eternally connected to her. She is the greater womb from whom we emerge and into whom we will be merged. Our earthly existence is nothing but a few days' interval on this planet in order to gain a different experience. Actually, we already have a destined home, and whenever we are in close communion with nature, quite surprisingly, we are just on the way to that eternal home.

So, whenever you feel any lack, never be disheartened; rather, come close to nature. She will never disappoint you. Smell those morning buds, talk to the leaves. You may learn from them how to transform and how to grow within. If possible, allow yourself to walk on the fields bare feet. Those grasslands may make you feel that you are a human being indeed, made of earthly soil and destined to merge into it. You are also grounded with your own roots, like the trees in those forests that are spreading out their branches up into the sky, evolving themselves, and at the same time remaining very much grounded with their own roots, with their own grace.

This communion with nature is not only a healing in itself; rather, it is a blessing from the supreme power of intelligence to help you find that inner child who still loiters within yourself, still desires love and adoration, and still has her presence beneath the hard layer of your conscious self; that childish self of your being who once used to wonder, gazing at the stars at night, and used to ask in utter astonishment, "Is this the exact way to communicate with heaven?"

I do not know whether it is the exact way to communicate with heaven or not. But I can assure you, my dear, that in close communion with nature, you can feel that bliss within. Your consciousness will introduce you to a different kind of realisation where, once again, you will be introduced to a different truth, a different reality that may help you to realise who you truly are. And then, quite naturally, you may start to realise that your existence is not temporal but eternal. And herein lies the mystery of our being, the mystery of our soul who always evolves, yearns for something new, but never leaves behind her eternal home.

"A thousand miles you've covered,
A thousand steps, I feel,
You may need to hover,
But your seed will remain the same,
And it does not need, I think,
That much technical frame.
But a mirror it needs to have
To hold the beauty within.
The beauty of this vast expansion,
Perhaps!
And to hold the truth
That still you have,
To feel this creation
As a magic of art,
As a mystery of eternity,
Where the stars still shine
With every beat of your heart!"

5 | Let's Stay Grounded and Evolve Yourself

In those early days of my childhood, when my innocence used to hark me back and inspire me to discover something unknown from that known world of Dos and Don'ts, I still remember that longing that I used to feel in those days. And that longing—I didn't know why I felt it—but it always had a tendency to bring me back under the starry sky in those nightly hours. I didn't know why, but the stillness and serenity of those nights attracted me a lot, and quite like a hypnotic spell, I used to stare at the sky overhead. Sometimes those glittering stars, shining and dazzling in their own beauty, sometimes that vast expansion used to beckon me to feel some special significance that amazed me greatly. Then I was barely five or six years old, and it was quite impossible for me to know how long those stars had been glittering in the sky, filling up the void with their dazzling presence, or how long they would continue to do so.

All through those nights, I used to wonder who lit up those stars every evening and quenched them early in the morning. I used to stare at them and hover around those thoughts every night, but found no answer satisfying my innocence. Sometimes I used to ask my mother. She never said anything, only smiled with her habitual sweetness.

During some of those nights, I also used to have an unnatural dream of losing myself in the midst of a dark tower. I still remember that dream vividly. The more I tried to find the exact passageway, the more I became trapped in those labyrinthine dark corridors. There was nothing but an all-enveloping darkness I could feel. There was no one to help me out of it. I tried to escape but found no one to hold my hand. And most of the time, that frightful dream kept me awake in the mid-hours of those nights, only to find myself trembling with fear and being consoled by my mother. I still remember her murmuring voice: "You need not worry, my dear. I'm always by your side to protect you, and will be, just like those silent stars dazzling and shining in the sky."

Sometimes my innocence used to trouble her late at night. "Do you know the name of that light man who lights up the stars at every dusk?" I would ask. She gently shook her head and replied with her habitual sweetness, "They don't need any light man, my dear! Rather, they have that power, that light within. But they do have a connection to their creator that always makes them shine with their own beauty, to light up the sky, to fill the void with an eternal truth, and that is a mystery."

For the next few years, I believed her every word until scientific reasoning entered my understanding and I got introduced to the analytical observations of my science books, from which I learnt about the components of those stars that make them shine brightly in the sky. But one thing I must tell you is that scientific knowledge never satisfied that longing I used to feel in those early days of my childhood.

I still remember those days of my early twenties, the days that used to inspire me to discover something different, yet significant and true to my existence. So, in search of that special something, whenever I found some respite from my habitual study hours, I used to stand alone in our garden to contemplate for a while, sometimes to perceive some greater truth that the stars of those evenings wanted to share with me. I used to stand still only to witness the evening darkness gradually descending upon the branches of that gigantic banyan tree in our garden.

Until my early teens, I used to wonder how it was possible for that tree to stay grounded through all the years, evolving at the same time despite enduring storms and darkness all alone. But now, with age, I can feel those mysteries—the mystery of that banyan tree, even the mystery of those stars that once filled my awareness with wonder and awe.

Here, in this chapter, I would like to share that mystery, that truth of our existence, that harmony and integrity of our being that connect us with our eternal strings, with that inner seed that we all have within us since eternity. And this truth is nothing but the truth of our being, and the truth of that eternal connection to our creator, who is always helping us to evolve and to transcend in newer ways, towards different territories where we can find that special significance, that special meaning of our existence, in spite of living in this mundane world, in spite of the darkness that usually frightens us.

When the Darkness within Introduces before You the Greater Womb, Your Origin

Most of the time, we tend to interpret darkness as incongruous or as something that cannot be explored properly, or in a way we usually wish to discover through our tangible perception. The dream that I used to have during those childhood nights was no exception. It was so frightful for me, something like losing myself in a mysterious, unfathomable dark dungeon from which escape could only be a myth for all. But what do you think — is that really the escape I was seeking for? According to the conscious interpretation of the mind, you may feel that it was just a normal dream experience that we all used to have in our childhood days, for in those days, more or less, we all suffered from an insecurity of losing ourselves from our secure shelter, the shelter of our parental home. So it is quite normal to have such dreams. But as days go on and circumstances change, we gradually start to feel that darkness not as something fearful but as something mysterious, which I somehow felt during my early teens, when the silent evening used to descend over the garden, covering that huge banyan tree.

You may think, "What is so unique about that? It is only a natural process to witness at dusk." In this connection, however, I would tell you that this natural process has some significance, some different meaning, and that meaning is somehow connected to your origin, to your depth. If you probe more deeply within, you may also feel that darkness is very much aligned with your being. At first, you may not recognise it; you may be a little bewildered and feel it as something incongruous, something terrible. But the reality is that it is the darkness from which you came and to which you need to return to be merged. It is the reality of your existence, the truth of your being. It is that place where your inner seed finds shelter to flourish once again. It is not darkness that holds you back and from which you just need to take refuge; it is the darkness that helps you to recognise your reality in a constructive way, in a way in which you can feel longing as a longing for something genuine, for creating something new. It is a mystery itself when darkness becomes the ground of your being, the reality of your existence as it is connected to your roots, your depth within. It is only through this darkness that you can feel where the truth of your existence lies.

When your suffering becomes unbearable and inconsolable, your ego can no longer handle such situations. At that point, you may start to feel that longing within, yet never find any answer. At the same time, you may feel that a new journey begins — a journey of probing deeper into the darkest regions of your existence, more like a spiritual quest than a journey in the ordinary sense. In the course of this new journey, some questions may come into your mind, such as "Who am I?", "Where did I come from?" or "Where should I go?" At this stage, I would tell you not to trouble yourself but to try to fathom deeply within with the help of these questions in a self-reflective manner. Try to perceive more deeply. Try to feel that eternal light surrounding the universe and your entity as well. If you probe further into the depth, you will find that descending into the darkness is not to lose yourself but to discover the ideal version of yourself, very much aligned with and true to that eternal womb within from which you emerged and into which you will be merged as an eternally blissful and spiritual being, in a natural way where the continuity of life is another form of transcending yourself and evolving your soul as well.

Ground Yourself with That Eternal Womb and Recognise Your True Self

I think by this time you have understood the point I was trying to convey at the very beginning of this chapter through that dream experience. Though on an apparent level it was just a feeling of insecurity experienced by a child's mind, if you probe deeper into that experience, you may feel that it was not a simple dream, but rather a longing, a quest to discover myself, a journey to recognise my true calling that was somehow connected to that dream where I lost myself in the midst of that darkness.

Most of the time we fear the unknown as something mysterious and compare it with unfathomable darkness without realising that probing into that darkness is essential to our growth, to recognising our true being, and to discovering that newness we all possess beneath the layers of our external conscious self. If you wish to know that secret code, you have to probe deeper within. Then that darkness may appear before you as a sort of revelation, a revelation that may help you to know the source of that light which helps the stars to dazzle in their own beauty since eternity. You may also feel that power which helps the banyan tree to stand all alone, in spite of the darkness and the storms, yet evolving at the same time, grounded by its own roots.

Most of the times we tend to interpret our downward journey as some sort of failure, while the upward movement is always considered an achievement. But if we wish to follow the footsteps of our soul, she will always lead us towards that dimension of our existence where being grounded is everything in knowing our true being, our true worth of living in this world. During this journey, as she leads you downward, you may feel baffled at times. You may not be able to identify exactly where she wishes to take you, as her true nature is not confined within a linear formation of categorisation, but is something beyond that, something that helps you to grow and transcend beyond this ordinary perception of living in this world.

During this journey, from the deeper roots of your heart, you may perceive where you need to crush your ego and where to surrender to the divine in order to feel the ideal essence of your being. And during this downward journey, you may perceive who your ideal soulmate is and recognise your eternal womb, from where you came and into which you will merge once more. Descending into the depths of your being, you will be able to know how and where she wishes to plant the seeds of faith and hope within you—seeds essential to perceiving your higher calling, that place where destiny waits to meet you.

Out of that darkness, you may realise that this dark night is nothing but the ultimate truth, the reality of your being. You may also interpret that darkness as the rich tapestry of your existence, where the art of your entity is to be carved out in its real nature, with that inner mystery that has always longed to evolve in a newer direction. Only then can you feel where lies the truth and beauty of that darkness, of that eternal womb that appeared before you as something frightful at first.

You may also realise the intrinsic message that the dream was trying to imprint upon my heart and soul during those childhood nights. Losing myself in that darkness was nothing but an opportunity from the divine to probe deeper into the depths and feel the ground of my being in a new way, where escaping from that darkness is not the reality, but probing deeper into it to find the truth is the reality itself. Descending into it, you may also perceive the true nature of your soul and what she is trying to whisper into your ears. You may stumble at times, may feel baffled descending into that depth, but at the same time, you may also feel her soft murmurings coming from the bottom of your heart:

Towards the darkest of the darks
When life may seem doomed and lost
Remember Me then, I may not appear before you
Quite like those morning hues
But my truth will help you see within, to find that light
That star to shine, fresh and pure
Quite like the morning dews, for sure.

When That Darkness within Encounters the Eternal Light of Truth and Wonder

In a deeper sense, I would say that this darkness is not something to be ignored or feared; rather, it is that phase of your life when you are eager to descend into the depths of your being. You may feel it as something mystical, but I would say that it is a phase of self-reflection, a stage of revelation where you can recognise your roots, your centre. It is your own longing to discover a deeper dimension of reality—the deeper dimension of your being. In that sense, whenever you are going through such dark phases of your life, remember one thing: this darkness is not something to be afraid of, but something that reminds you of your own worth—your worth as an entity, your worth as a spiritual being.

In that sense, it may be felt that this darkness serves only to help you comprehend the truth of your being. At this juncture, your external conscious self may stumble at first, but at the same time, you cannot ignore that higher calling coming from the bottom of your heart. Once again, you may fall into the trap of that dilemma—whether to rise high or to channelize your consciousness downward. But if you wish to remain true to yourself, you cannot deny the call of your heart, and quite naturally, you may feel that you are descending downward just to receive the call of your destiny—to mould the clay of your entity in a newer and more creative way.

Descending into this darkness not only helps you grow psychologically but also helps you transcend, to know your worth as a true spiritual being. It is nothing but a deeper exploration within yourself and a knowing of the truth and harmony of your being that is eternally connected to that universal intelligence, not only surrounding your existence but also the entire creation as well.

Herein lies the true worth of surrender, where surrendering yourself to that darkness, to that eternal womb, may lead your consciousness towards that unknown territory of harmony and truth. After knowing the reality of your being, you may start to feel peace and bliss within. You may also perceive the true power of higher consciousness that is deeply aligned with that spiritual dimension from where you may recall your home once again—under the perception of eternity, where the mystery of this darkness may not be interpreted as something pessimistic, but as something deeply attuned to your soul, your inner essence that always speaks to you: how to know yourself, how to know that beauty and wonder you possess within, under the shell of your conscious self.

Finding Your Centre Is the Happiest Way to Transcend and Evolve Yourself

During those days of my early teens, while I used to walk through the labyrinthine passages of our garden, I sometimes felt a communion with that huge banyan tree. It was not its size that attracted me so much; rather, it was the mystery within it that always inspired me to open my heart in order to perceive something greater than this tangible world of interpretations—something different from those scientific observations with which we are accustomed on a daily basis.

I did not know what I used to gain from that communion, but I certainly felt something intangible—peaceful enough to transcend my consciousness to a different realm, from where I did not receive anything tangible, but could discover a newer identity that I already had within, though I had kept it unnoticed in the daily course of my life. That identity was something like an interconnectedness with my own roots, quite like that banyan tree—staying grounded in its own roots but evolving at the same time in its own beauty and helping me to feel the existence I have, since eternity.

I think most of you have understood my point. The longing that I had since my childhood was not for anything tangible, but for something deeply aligned with my roots—connected to that 'inner seed' that we all have within. Yet, remaining unaware that we are eternally connected to some universal creative force surrounding our being as well as the entire creation, we tend to indulge in dilemmas. Nowadays, most of the problems arise from this ignorance—that we are eternal entities connected to a higher force. But I must tell you that herein lies the efficacy of that darkness, and the value of probing more deeply into it, into the depth of your being, in order to recognise your true home, the eternal womb, and the true meaning of reconciling with your eternal mate.

This reconciliation not only helps you to grow psychologically, but it also helps you to evolve and emerge with your true spiritual nature, very much akin to your higher self, very much aligned to the depth of your being that quite spontaneously inspires you to be the sculptor of your own being, in order to be that creative artist who knows the true worth of emergence. This descent into the depths not only helps you to get a proper self-reflection, but also inspires you to accept who you really are and wherein lies your true endeavour. But if you are unable to probe into the depths only because of that darkness, you are not only hindering your path of emergence, but also blocking yourself from being true to your being.

Descending down into the depth is not only a spontaneous way of recognising yourself, but it is also your soul's yearning to transform yourself into a newer way. But most of us cannot recognise it properly and tend to see this darkness as a black monster engulfing our being and withdrawing us from the colours and magic of life. But I would remind you that here at this juncture, we misinterpret this downward journey and once again fall into the trap of that false ego, remaining completely unaware of the fact that this yearning of our soul is nothing but a means to bring self-awareness within ourselves to know our true colour, our destiny for which we are born on this planet. The encounter with this darkness is nothing but a call from your soul to shed off your old skin through this deeper probing and evolve once again, keeping yourself completely aligned to the roots, to that 'inner seed' you have within.

It is another way of finding your centre, which you have lost in the course of your survival, and which most of the time appears to you as a hopeless existence. But if you pause for a while and allow yourself to go deeper, you can feel that darkness is nothing but the inner power you have. It is that corrective force of your heart, reminding you once again of your true worth and trying to pull you back towards that higher calling you are destined for. And in the course of descending into the depths, you can perceive that it is not darkness but a guiding force within you, walking down the streets with you, making you feel that your existence has some special significance and that your life has some special meaning to sustain.

I am not that darkness that pulls you downward
Makes you feel how feeble, timid, you are
But that darkness instead brings you back
To see within, to feel the sunrise, to have that gaze
That once you longed for
As your eternal grace.

When Surrender to Your Roots Becomes the Only Way to Evolve Yourself

That dream of losing myself in that dark dungeon was nothing but a serendipitous encounter with my own being, which somehow inspired me to recognise my worth and evolve in accordance with that higher call. It was a call to surrender myself to that darkness within, surrendering my entity to that truth of my existence where I may find no one but only eternity as my guide and mate.

Whenever you are surrendering yourself to your roots, your centre, remember one thing: you are also surrendering to that universal, divine intelligence, that anchoring power of your life, creative and responsible enough not only to heal you psychologically but also to help you grow spiritually. This is a way of nurturing yourself once again, true to the essence of your soul, and evolving yourself toward those highest ideals where, in spite of darkness, you will be able to bring your sculptor back to fill the void in your life with higher wisdom and newer hope. And here, once again, you can feel the truth and harmony of your being, harking you back and inspiring you to listen more creatively to your soul's voice within.

It is not a wonder to feel Me within,
Within that darkness that harks you back,
But the wonder is to feel that light that you still have
In spite of my darkness;
You still have that magic lamp, shining and gleaming within,
Perhaps to share a story
That harks you back, maybe trying to tell you the truth,
The truth to bring you back,
The truth to show you a different way
Where eternity still holds your hand.

6 | Accept Who You Are and Feel the Bliss Within

In today's world of materialistic needs and aspirations, the word *acceptance* may seem to you to be something unrealistic. You may think that accepting where you are or who you are is nothing but presenting yourself before the world as someone who does not have any option to grow up, rather than accepting who they are. In this world of so-called success where we are constantly compared by an invisible, parametric success meter, it is becoming impossible for us, day by day, to distinguish between what we truly want and what we truly need. We are even unable to differentiate between the real and the unreal. All the time, our expectations tempt us to search for something better that sometimes does not fit in the world of our reality.

But most of the time, in this course of searching, we not only disrespect our inner strength but also frustrate ourselves once again and lure ourselves into falling under the trap of numerous illusions and disillusionments. In this course of searching for something better, quite unknowingly, we start to decide our goals, set up our yardsticks and allow our minds to seek external appreciation according to that so-called parametric success meter. Quite unconsciously, we present ourselves before a mirror that is actually set up by external viewers. This is the biggest mistake we make every now and then, becoming victims of instant comparisons and, sometimes, of shallow gratifications.

Quite automatically, we start to believe that we do not have any real worth within. Rather, we are nothing but simple human machines comparing ourselves with others according to that so-called success meter, expecting something bigger that actually has no value in the true core of our existence.

Here, in this chapter, I would like to remind you that you are not a simple human being but have some eternal power within. And herein lies the greatest role of acceptance: to bring that strength back into your entity in order to ground your being in your true self, without any expectations or grievances. The moment you start to accept whoever you are, quite automatically your ego sheds off and you start to feel that you are aligning yourself with the deeper part of your psyche that is eternal and beyond any form of tangible perception. Gradually, you may start to realise that you are not a single entity but a spiritual being with a divine truth.

But this is possible only when you are able to perceive your true entity and can accept yourself with the openness of your heart and the serenity of your soul. I know that is not an easy task to accomplish. But I must assure you that it is also not an impossible one if you still have that urge to know yourself, your true identity, and have the strength to feel the eternal bliss that you already have within. Non-acceptance only makes you grieve over something that really does not exist or belong to you in this real world of your existence. But most of the time, we fail to understand this simple truth of life and tend to misinterpret the ideal core of reality, allowing ourselves once again to indulge in the worldly pleasures of the senses and material needs, entirely forgetting what our soul needs in order to heal herself.

Acceptance does not mean losing your faith altogether or accepting everything that is going on with a passive understanding. Rather, acceptance means trusting the process and allowing your soul to believe in divine guidance and transcend your consciousness to that level from where life may not seem to you as only a fruitless survival, but as something through which you can feel the eternal grace and bliss within.

Accepting Who You Are Is Becoming Aware of Your Strengths and Weaknesses

Do you know where the root cause of our suffering lies? It is all because of our ignorance, I feel. Most of the time, we are ignorant of who we truly are. Our desires and wishes often lead us towards a state of dilemma and confusion where we fail to relate to ourselves, to that truth we already have within, and consequently fail to relate to the world outside. We search from one place to another, sometimes hoping for something better, sometimes even depriving ourselves of self-respect, but never feeling satisfied enough, never finding that peace of mind we are seeking. The more we indulge in that pursuit, the more we find that we are trapping ourselves once again in a never-ending, labyrinthine dark dungeon. And every time, we fail to connect with that inner truth that we have within since the primordial time of our existence. We even fail to perceive that we are already complete within and need not search for that completeness around any external corner. Rather, what we need to do is realise our individual identity and accept ourselves with all our grace, with all our faults, along with our tears and laughter, along with our uniqueness and shortcomings.

Here, I would like to tell you that having ambitions and pursuing them is not wrong if you are striving for what you are destined to be. But if you are running after something that does not fit your real self, then I think it may become a little problematic for you to trust the process. And here once again comes the dilemma and confusion. At that very moment, your desires may tempt you to follow the path of external appreciation, keeping you completely unaware of the fact that your soul needs to have some other options, some other ways to flourish. And here once again we lose ourselves and quite automatically prove to be ordinary slaves to our never-ending expectations, completely ignoring the reality that we are already complete within ourselves, with all our graceful and darker shades of existence. That is why we do not need to search for any other place. Indeed, we are already at that place, already with every possibility that our soul needs to rejuvenate and flourish. But most of the time, we forget this simple truth and push ourselves towards that region of comparison, according to that so-called parametric success meter.

Actually, success does not come to those who always deny their real selves. The more we deny ourselves, the more we become alienated from our ideal self, resulting in frustration and allowing ourselves to fall into the trap of dissatisfaction and existential crisis. As a result, quite unconsciously, we become overwhelmed and present ourselves before the world as creatures who only know how to imitate others, frustrating themselves through the tools of external imitation and comparison.

To put it simply, I would like to remind you that we are all individually unique. We cannot be compared with one another, and accepting who we truly are helps us to understand that unique individuality. Moreover, through this acceptance, I feel you may gain an alternative insight even though your shortcomings. But never feel disheartened; rather, accept those flaws with an open heart. Accept them as something truly yours, rather than being depressed. Try to find alternative ways to feel your presence. Do not live others' lives, lamenting over what you do not have; rather, try to appreciate what you still have and work on that.

Herein lies the grace of being accepted by yourself. I think it may not bring you that so-called success that most of us seek, but it can help you understand who you truly are and can bring solace within, helping you to perceive the real truth of your existence. The moment you realise the simple truth of your life, you will start to feel where real success lies. You may start to explore the eternal rhythm of your life itself, and then all the complexes, involvements and expectations will quite automatically start to fade away. You will become aware of the fact that you are being introduced to a different reality where being disillusioned and disheartened by the external world is not only unwelcome but also a barrier to recognising yourself and your inner worth. Your real self may not be a favourite with everyone, but if you have faith in yourself, you will come to know that the magic of acceptance lies within. You will realise that, whatever the circumstances, you need to accept the process and the divine guidance that continually guides this entire creation, along with your existence. Then you need not worry at all about what others feel about you. If you know your strengths and weaknesses, your inner worth and the truth within your being, you will quite naturally start to feel the power of your soul and perceive where she prefers to lead you. Trust me, this entire process is quite magical. And this magic starts to happen the moment you start to explore yourself and align with the truth you have within, since the primordial time of your existence.

I feel acceptance does nothing but motivate you to live in the present moment, letting you breathe freely in a spontaneous way and helping you to grow within, in order to welcome a new dawn that will accept your identity the way you are. The more you accept who you are, the more you will align not only with the truth you have within but also with the universal truth of life itself, which never permits you to see yourself as timid, craving for something you are not destined for. Rather, it always guides you towards an alternative way of finding your centre. There, you don't need to be ashamed or think of others' appreciation, but can feel that you also have a special purpose on this planet and that you are only a spiritual being (predestined, I mean to say) in a human form — nothing more, nothing less than that. This awareness, quite surprisingly, helps you to understand that your presence is eternal, beyond any external appreciation, beyond any external judgement, beyond anything that makes you feel you are not good enough.

And reaching up to this point of realisation, you will be able to perceive where the true meaning of your life. You will understand that comparison and non-acceptance can only lead you towards a stage of unfulfilled ambition, while acceptance helps you to feel serenity within, even if you have not achieved that so-called success in your life. Life is not about achievements and great ambitions; rather, it is about sitting for a while, allowing your heart to listen to the soft murmurings of your soul, and transcending your consciousness to that level where expectations have no room. Then only acceptance brings before you that special mirror to behold the beauty that you already have within.

Acceptance Always Leads You towards a State of Self-Reflection

Though on an apparent level of understanding, you may feel that acceptance does nothing but simply helps you to go with the flow in a passive way, at this juncture, I would like to remind you that acceptance is not a state of being passive. Rather, it has an infinite potential to transcend your consciousness into a different state of realisation. Then you may come to know that the part of you which is running after external satisfactions is not the real you, but a false, illusory part of your shadow self that does not allow you to see the real beauty within yourself. Under its hypnotic spell, you can do nothing but run after something that actually has no reality at the core of your existence.

As a result, the more you get involved into those external things, the more resentful and bitter you start to become, completely negating the rhythm of nature, the rhythm of life itself. Quite unknowingly, you start to block the path of your inner realisation. The more you indulge in those external things, ignoring the real core of your existence, the more you negate the rhythm of universal creative intelligence. The reality is not in those external things you are running after, but in the Truth you have within. To explore that reality, that truth within, I feel you need to accept yourself and surrender to the divine intelligence that governs the entire universe without any pause or complaint. A genuine acceptance of your heart has the magical power to bring awareness within yourself. The moment you become aware of who you are, trust me, that is the moment when your being connects to the divine intelligence, for you are not separated from it. At this very moment, you become aligned with your inner purpose, which is essential to communicate with yourself and with the world outside in order to lead your life and take responsibility in a more relevant and practical way.

To explain this in a simpler way, I would like to share with you an extraordinary experience that happened to a lady who was utterly on the verge of depression and had even decided to leave this world forever. But something magical happened to her that completely changed her way of thinking and, quite surprisingly, inspired her to lead her life more blissfully, not according to the whims of others who had tried to change her altogether, but according to the spontaneous rhythm of her soul, which knows how to heal and how to grow within. I feel her words will certainly fill your heart with awe and inspiration and help you to perceive the wonder that acceptance can create in one's being;

"It was those days when there was nothing left to lose for me except that unfortunate life I was dragging behind, except those sorrows I was brooding over. Life seemed to me a mockery of my own. My fragile self used to sneer at me every night. I used to crawl every day, crawled with my inabilities, crawled with those unfulfilled ambitions that used to pop into my mind every day and night. Starkly, I felt that I had been drowning in a dark dungeon of uncertainties, finding no one to help me out. I was totally unable to accept my helplessness. The reality, the unfortunate incident that happened to me, always seemed to me like some mockery, a trick that life played on me! All the time, I used to feel that nothing worse could happen when someone loses her entire

possessions, her social reputation and everything that is essential to make one stable and confident enough to sustain in this tough world of existence where everyone prefers to judge you according to your external position. However glossy and sparkling it seems to be, whether it fits with your real self or not, people always love to notice those external parameters. But unfortunately, that superficially glossy external shell was not available to me right at that moment when life played that trick on me.

But years later, I realised that my suffering was not for that loss, rather for the non-acceptance of my real self that had been continually stressing me out and distracting me from my ideal purpose. In those days, I used to gaze at the sky, at those twinkling stars. I did not know why, but somehow I started to feel the stillness of those nights within. I started to feel that my entire entity had been gradually aligned with that nocturnal beauty, and a surrender was needed, I deeply felt, a surrender to the divine intelligence and accepting everything that happened to me in those past few years. And trust me, dear, the moment I started to accept myself, quite surprisingly, I started to feel a different meaning of my existence. I started to be aware of some blissful energy surrounding not only my entity, but also the entire universe, which I had been ignoring when I used to complain of my circumstances.

That was a different realisation, something that cannot be expressed in words but can only be felt within, and somehow, I started to feel that I need not brood over those past sorrows or indulge my ego all the time to gain some external appreciation and allow those external whims and tricks to control me. Rather, what I need to do is only to surrender, surrender to that nocturnal beauty, surrender to the stillness of those nights, surrender to that absolute silence and moreover to that divine intelligence, responsible for the entire creation and my existence as well. And at that very moment, that nocturnal beauty somehow, I felt, started to appear before me as a mirror itself to hold the beauty I have within, since the primordial time of my existence. And I started to feel that it was not only a simple mirror, but has a magical healing power in itself, to heal all the wounds and to help me to feel once again the eternal grace that I have within. It was really a different realisation that, at the very first place, startled me at once, but gradually helped me a lot to perceive the inner beauty, the inner purpose I am destined for. And an eternal truth I perceived that night: the truth is not of gaining something external, rather the truth is understanding myself, becoming compassionate to my failures and embracing my success with the truthful openness of my heart. As acceptance, I feel, has only that power to make you believe that you are not a single entity, rather an entity aligned to the entire universe. So we need not complain, need not remorse over the pasts, but what we need to do is only to accept, to love ourselves, with whatever faults or grace we have."

You may think, what exactly made that lady change her perspective altogether? At this juncture, I would like to remind you that nothing tangible happened. But the real magic happened within herself. The moment she started to accept whoever she is, quite surprisingly, her unconscious began to respond constructively, allowing her consciousness to open a new vista for knowing herself, and she realised quite automatically where lies her soul's purpose. And it all happened the moment she started to accept herself, with all her grace and follies, with all her success and misfortunes. As by that time, she got realized where she may have that inner peace, where she once again may feel that she`s all alive with her grace, with her presence!

Here lies the true worth of accepting yourself, the true purpose of surrendering your entity completely to the divine intelligence, not only to know yourself, but to explore the inner enigma that still throbs within you, to feel that unexplored purity we all have, within, but always tend to avoid in the pursuit of seeking something external. While the actual reality of life lies in the total acceptance of who you are, allowing your consciousness to perceive that truth, within.

Accepting Who You Are Is Healing Yourself and Strengthening the Phoenix Within

Do you ever know the actual cause of your suffering and the sense of lack that you feel most of the time, even when you've gained everything and are relishing your tangible success, being at the top of your so-called success meter? I feel the lack you're experiencing every now and then does not come from your external self; rather, it arises from the inner core of your psyche that has somehow become alienated from the truth within. This is not the suffering of your external self but the suffering of your soul, which needs to be healed.

The moment you start to reject yourself is the moment you begin to collapse the spontaneous flow of your soul, which is very much independent in nature. However dark the realities may seem, your soul always has the power to evolve in a spontaneous way, to heal those wounds, and to help you realise that the crisis you're suffering from is not an external one but arises from your non-acceptance of who you truly are. On the contrary, the moment you start to recognise yourself, you quite automatically become more compassionate towards yourself. You may begin to feel that you are not only recognising yourself in a different way but also healing yourself, speaking with your inner depth. And herein lies the need to understand and love yourself as you are.

A few years back, quite unexpectedly, I met a lady of about fifty-one years of age who had once been a successful IT professional but was then running her own bakery shop in Bangalore. Quite accidentally, I stumbled across her shop, and through a couple of interactions, I came to know a secret of her life. That secret was that, even when she was at the peak of her professional success, she had never been satisfied within. All the time, a sense of lack hovered around her. Do you want to know what that lack was about? I would like to share her own confession:

It was a prison for me. Sometimes it felt somewhat claustrophobic. I achieved everything in my life — name, fame, and success — except peace! The more I got involved in those external appreciations, the more I started to feel that I was not only denying my self-worth but also entering into a dark dungeon from which escape was possible only when I accepted myself the way I am, leaving behind the life of servitude, the life of expectations from the outside world. And this realisation didn't come to me overnight. I contemplated it, perceived the depth within, and decided to emerge before the world as my soul wished me to be — peaceful, satisfied, and grounded in the truth and reality I have within. Some of you may sneer at me, may think how foolish I was to quit that job earning dollars to become a simple bakery shop owner. But trust me, dear, here I found the peace, satisfaction, and integrity I never discovered in that high-profile job. I'm not criticising them; they are themselves. But I also needed to be myself. I needed to accept myself what I am.

I think this is an excellent example of accepting the truth you have within, negating all the fears of what might happen if the world does not accept you. If you accept yourself as you are, there is no need for any external approval. Herein lies the truth of your existence, the truth of your being, the true emergence of your soul. Though the above experience holds true for that lady, I am not suggesting that all of you should follow in her footsteps. Everyone in this world has a different experience, a different story to tell, and a different truth to handle. So let us ask our inner selves, speak with them in silence, and allow our consciousness to choose the right path, one that aligns with our real selves.

Trust me, the moment you start to accept yourself, quite unknowingly, you begin to strengthen your inner phoenix that we all have within, but often tend to ignore. Acceptance does nothing but lead your consciousness to understand yourself in a different way and to find the divine light within, helping you realise that your existence is not temporal but carries the truth of eternity itself.

In simpler terms, acceptance prepares us to confront the life lessons we generally tend to ignore in our day-to-day lives. It has a marvellous, magical power not only to open our hearts and help us explore our individual identities but also to make us perceive that we are predestined spiritual beings in our earthly existence. I feel this understanding is deeply relevant to healing ourselves, gaining better insight, and emerging before the world true to our being, forming a wonderful relationship with ourselves where depth speaks to depth, negating everything external that may hinder our soul's path to flourish.

I feel this genuine love and acceptance naturally heal all the wounds we suffer from. Quite automatically, we begin to feel the presence of that eternal truth we have within us since the primordial time of our existence. Gradually, we recognise the ground of our being. Faith arises naturally to help us, and once again, we are introduced to our creator, to the phoenix we have within. Perhaps it is to enable us to emerge before the world in a new and creative way — one that may not be acceptable to all, but when it is acceptable to the core of our being, to that inner self to which we return again and again, only then are we able to maintain balance within, negating disequilibrium and aligning with our true selves.

Accepting and Finding the Truth Within Is the Ideal Way to Feel Eternal Bliss

I feel your denial to accept yourself is nothing but one of the causes of your spiritual deprivation, an alienation from your centre within, and consequently, facing a crisis that continually leads you towards a state of mental disequilibrium. The moment you start to deny yourself, remember that is the moment when you become alienated from this universal source of energy. At the same time, you start to ignore your very presence, the truth you have within that is not temporal but has eternal significance to your existence.

In this connection, I would like to remind you that your thought is essential to lead your consciousness in a fruitful way. If you are constantly thinking negatively, seeking appreciation from others, and dwelling on thoughts of discontent, despair, anxiety and non-acceptance, you may never be able to find that peace within. You may never perceive the true meaning of your aliveness. And if you fail to do so, you will automatically be unable to relate to yourself and to the world outside. Accepting yourself and communicating with your inner being are essential to feel the bliss of eternity within. Accepting yourself is not only to understand who you are, but to perceive the truth within, sense your presence, accept your eternal entity as a whole and realise your inner purpose on this earth — the purpose of your existence.

It heals your soul, making you realise that the meaninglessness you are facing within is not caused by any external deprivation but by alienation from your spiritual centre within. And I think the cause of your suffering is more because of this spiritual deprivation rather than any psychological upheaval. The more you choose the path of non-acceptance, the more you choose to be deprived, both psychologically and spiritually. Acceptance can bring you to that stage of self-reflection where you may have that pure consciousness to find the light within. It will help you to feel the distinction between your real self and the self that you have as the external layer of your conscious mind, enabling you to gain that higher knowledge in order to lead your consciousness towards a state where you need not be bothered about what others think of you, but may feel the deeper truth of your existence — the most loving truth of humanity itself. And that truth is accepting who you are and accepting the world as it is, not taking drastic measures to change others, but choosing to evolve within and relate to the world outside in an insightful way.

Acceptance will help you choose the path where your inner self alone knows how to speak and what to say from the depths within. And trust me, the language your deeper self knows is not like the one your conscious self uses every now and then. It is something higher, something to contemplate. And herein lies its healing effect, its magical power to bring you back to your centre, to your home, recognising the ground of your being and realising where lies the power to feel the bliss within. Trust me, the moment you start to accept who you are, quite automatically, all those negative thoughts that you used to dwell on will start to fade away, and you will start to realise your inner experiences, start to believe that you are an eternal entity, and are grounded and true to your being. Only then may you feel where lies the worth of your true emergence before the world and how you can feel that everlasting bliss within.

You may also start to feel how it is possible in this tangible world to accept everything and be blissful all the time. At this juncture, I would remind you that acceptance not only frees you from your ego, allowing your consciousness to transcend beyond this realm of tangible understanding, but also opens up your heart's space and allows your soul to evolve once again according to her own choice. And the moment you start to realise that you are a spiritual being, quite magically you start to feel that eternal bliss within—the bliss of your presence. And herein lies the beauty and purity of your existence, the feeling that acceptance can bring into your mind and soul where the priority will be only your blissful existence, not the boundaries or conditions that people generally set up for you.

And herein lies the feeling of bliss, like that of an innocent child who knows no boundaries but only knows how to surrender and how to accept the way he or she is. This is the purest form of bliss that you can experience when you start to accept yourself for who you are in a real sense. And I think this is the ideal realisation that may help you grow within and regain the confidence you have lost by comparing yourself to external parameters. Generally, we lose our confidence whenever we fail to realise ourselves and become disconnected from the universal source of energy. As a consequence, we gradually lose our ground of being and once again fall into the trap of hopelessness instead of seeking the purest light within. Having satisfaction and feeling the bliss within is not only a temporal matter to understand. Rather, I feel this bliss is already within you. But in the course of complaining about your inner worth, you may have forgotten that you also have that divinity within. And this is the only way to free yourself from all such negative thoughts and enlighten your soul to that level from where life may not seem to you only a complaining journey with some hopeless survivors, but a blissful and soulful one to continue.

You Need Not Be Frightened Enough
Facing those darker hours when time seems to you
Like a ceasing monster, a heartless giant to crush your power,
Instead, choose to see the happy sunrise that never complains
For its early rise.
Choose to see those blooming flowers, dangling their heads,
Maybe to make a happy bower,
But never perplexed themselves,
Never asked others for help,
But always keep their faith alive and accept their destiny,
That they are here for a wonderful life;
Accept their destiny that they are here and will be
Just to make us feel that we too are nothing
But only some humans,
Eternally predestined.

7 | You May Be Lonely but Not Alone

If you're considering yourself as one of those hopeless beings, surviving in this world where no one is accepting you for who you are and only making you feel that you're in this world merely to lead your life as some lonely wanderer, alone and helpless, let me tell you that here, in this chapter, I'm not going to criticise those people who are making you feel that you're not worthy enough to be with anyone or pushing you towards that dark territory of loneliness. Instead, my purpose here is to make you feel that you may be lonely at some phases of your life when time may come and make you feel that your existence is nothing but a confinement amidst some unavoidable circumstances. But never lose your faith at that very moment; rather, try to feel what exactly those circumstances are trying to tell you. If you pay heed to that, you may hear a gentle voice whispering:

You're not alone, my dear! Prepare yourself for another goal, for another mission where you need not feel that you're helpless and alone!

Being in Solitude Is Another Way to Expand Your Consciousness

During the time of loneliness, you may feel you're the most hopeless one in the world. You find no one to converse with, no one to care for you. You feel like nothing but an inessential earthly body with no ground to sustain in this world. This loneliness may haunt you every now and then. You may also experience some existential crisis within. Sometimes your survival self may grieve over that loneliness and ask you, in a fit of desperation, "Is this the ideal way we ever promised to live?" But if you pause for a while and allow your inner self to perceive, you may feel the presence of a resting dove within. Then loneliness may not appear to you as a confinement, but as a blessing in disguise, helping you reinterpret yourself in a newer way and rediscover an eternal truth that this loneliness is trying to permeate, despite all the oddities and crises around you. And at that very moment, you may also feel some gentle whispers coming from the depths of your being. You may startle for a moment and find no one around the corner, but you can feel someone's gentle presence within, inspiring you to move forward, whispering into your ears:

The wind may be rough,
So is the path, you stumble at every moment.
I know you're stuck, but have you ever felt
Where is this solitude guiding you to halt?

You may feel rejected and abandoned, just like a wounded warrior waiting on that desolate island of loneliness, but if you probe deeper into your being, you may feel an enigmatic presence of something higher that only this loneliness has brought before you. When you're feeling lonely under the dark blue sky on some grieving night, just try to feel the wilderness of that night, her calmness, and her enigmatic presence. At first, you may not perceive anything special. But if you pause for a while to feel that calmness, you may realise that this wilderness carries a message within it—a message of the inherent truth of our existence—a truth that uncovers the mystery of our loneliness. It not only allows our consciousness to expand its horizon into a different realm but also enables our being to feel that this dark night is nothing but a period of restoration, of healing our wounds and preparing ourselves for a better tomorrow, for a newer dawn. Here, the nightly silence is not to be felt as something of despair, but as something of higher wisdom that gently comes with her tiny steps only to make you feel that you're not alone, but that you're here on this planet to explore the depth of your being and reinterpret something higher that you've not yet found while roaming along those overcrowded streets.

When Loneliness Empowers You to Keep Alive Your Faithful Imagination

I feel loneliness is nothing but an opportunity from the divine to centre your being and explore that inner seed that has been flourishing within you since the primordial time of your existence. This will always make you believe that there has always been a divine intelligence by your side to protect you and to make you feel that your existence is truly precious and eternally connected to the universe. So how can you be so lonely when the entire universe is by your side?

And this is exactly what happened to a middle-aged woman in our surroundings who never allowed herself to believe that she was going through any crisis. Instead, every night before she went to sleep, she used to write emails and send them to her own inbox. Do you want to know what those emails were about? They were just some simple "thank you" messages to her soulmate that she used to send to herself. At first, it seemed quite surprising to us when she told us about this extraordinary habit of sending herself emails every single night. But a few months later, we discovered the real mystery hidden in it.

Though at first glance it may seem to you to be only some messages of love and affection written for her loved one, do you know who that loved one was? If you probe deeper, you may perceive that her soulmate was no one but someone very special who had always been with her since eternity, listening to her every word, reading her every email, downloading every detail and writing back to her in order to make her feel she was not alone. You may say that this was just a vague imagination, but I would rather interpret it as a faithful imagination of her heart, an imagination that was coming from the depth of her being.

And there, this faithful imagination was enough for her not only to sustain herself but to live with her true mate and to believe in that divine magic surrounding the universe. That was the ideal magic that always foretells the truth of our existence. The truth where we can never feel alone, but rather see it as a blessing in disguise to evolve in a new way, quite like that lonely woman for whom the period of loneliness came as a phase of self-reflection, not to brood over her sorrows but as a period of rejuvenation to restore her inner balance, to feel the depth of her being in spite of the darkness, and to rise once again like the phoenix from the ashes.

When Loneliness Helps You to Heal and Enlighten Yourself in a Different Way

Those of you who are thinking that this lady must be someone very selfish, and that's why fate had played its tricks with her, leaving her lonely forever, only with her own laptop and mailbox to chat with, let me assure you that the reality was not like that, but rather far more tragic to be healed and overcome by someone else. That process of writing something, opening her mail account and sending those to her own was nothing but quite like a painkiller for her to heal those wounds of loneliness she was going through during that tough period. It not only made her feel that she was not alone, but also helped her to perceive the greater truth of her existence, the truth where being alone was not a punishment from God, but an opportunity to have a self-revelation, to experience that strength within to enlighten herself in order to live, to create a newer version of herself when she had nothing but only darkness ahead.

It would be utterly impossible for anyone to believe that she was going through that crisis of loneliness on the very first meeting with her. And my experience was also not exceptional in that regard. It was only through her own expressions during one of those casual chats that we occasionally used to have on some leisurely afternoons that I got to know how those days of loneliness had completely changed her vision and empowered her soul to flourish within, helping her to evolve in a newer way in order to be aligned with her true purpose.

Here I'm giving you some of her experiences that she shared with me at our last meeting:

I accept that I'm lonely. And I'm thankful for that. And I'm also grateful that I've this loneliness around me. At least I'm not surrounded by those fake ones. But trust me, I'm not alone! I know life mocks me, sometimes sneers and howls at me. People scorn, calling me 'a helpless creature!' But I've never complained, never tried to explain myself anywhere else. Instead, I always choose to be silent, as I know I'm very much with myself and moreover have an eternal mate to talk with. Every night, I open my mailbox, type something, some messages that only a thankful heart may express to her beloved, and send those to my own mail account. You may think that all these are such nonsense that I'm talking about. But trust me, dear, I've been doing this for quite a long time. And I've a deep belief in my heart that all my mails are being received and downloaded by that eternal mate, guiding and protecting me since the primordial time. Whenever I keep myself engaged in this task of sending those mails to my own mailbox, I never feel that loneliness or that grief inside. Instead, I always feel a higher level of consciousness inspiring me to expand my vision, to feel the calmness of that resting dove sleeping within my entity since eternity.

She never took that loneliness as her failure, but as a spiritual quest, and there came an exploration, a self-reflection. It was very much evident through her own speech. Instead of brooding over that loneliness, she preferred to use that period of solitude with all her grace and gratitude, only to witness those wonderful miracles that were coming her way. Do you want to know what exactly happened to her? That loneliness ultimately channelized her intuition towards a different realm and inspired her to embark on a newer journey to write down a memoir of her own, using all the wisdom and experiences that she gained during that tough period of loneliness.

And truly it helped her to emerge in a newer way, as an empowered soul who knows the true worth of her life, where being lonely doesn't mean that someone is alone, rather it means that he or she has some higher power inside to connect to the entire universe and feel the divine magic within, even while living in this tangible world of mundane reality. I know you're eager enough to know what exactly she used to write, opening her own mailbox and sending it to herself, that ultimately led her to decide to publish her own memoir. I can only give you some of those messages, and I feel that would be enough for you to see where she got the strength not only to survive all alone in this world, but also to contemplate and lead herself towards a new meaning of existence. Some of her emails were like:

"Thanks for listening to me. I know you care for me, you love me, whoever I am and whatever I've with me. I know you loved me during those happy hours or those moments when I had nothing but only to confront those lonely towers! I know you love me during those fearful nights when only the owl hoots and knows my plight, or during those early morns when the birds leave their nests to have some extra grains. I know you love me during those crowded mornings or during those lonely nights when I see no one else but only you to feel my plight!"

These were all the thankful messages that she used to send to her own mailbox every night. Never think that I'm also suggesting you do that every night whenever you feel lonely, because those were all her own personal manifestations, her personal belief to find her eternal mate by her side. But I must tell you, whenever you feel those dark clouds of loneliness trying to blur your vision, just have a deep faith inside that you're being watched over by some eternal energy, divine and magical. So nothing ill can harm you as long as you're connected to that universal intelligence. Wherever you go, whenever you feel lonely, that divine intelligence will always be by your side as your soul mate, or like that mate who is with you and will be forever, beyond these mundane hours of birth and death.

8 | Let's Descend More into the Dark and Find Out That Secret Code

It was really a journey for me; the more I descended into those dark passageways, the more I felt something different—something intangible yet mysterious and powerful. Somehow, I felt that I was not only descending into those dark passageways, but also into the depths of something else, into the depths of some mystery, where I might find a different truth, perhaps the truth of my existence. At first, I was startled and felt trapped in those dark passageways. But as I descended further into those dark and secret corridors of that unending, lonely tower, I started to feel that I was there for a reason, perhaps to explore something beyond this world of tangibility, yet something very much aligned with the ideal core of reality, with eternity itself. And I started to feel the mystery within, and an inner depth within myself, which, quite surprisingly, began to whisper in an inaudible way. But there was something special in its inaudibility that jolted me at once, and in the midst of that darkness, somehow I found myself introduced to my greater womb, from where I came and into which I will be merged someday.

You may startle a bit, pause for a while and ask yourself: is this the ideal way to be introduced to the origin of your existence? Or is this only a mystic experience that one can have while going through some crisis? Actually, this experience was nothing but a dream that a painter had on a single night, and he shared it with me when I was in Pondicherry a few years back.

Quite accidentally, I stumbled across him while strolling along the beach during a morning walk, and after only a couple of conversations, I got to know about his dream experiences from those days. Sometimes, he also dreamed of a dark and lonely tower where he was trapped, searching for help but finding no one to free him from that painful experience. Sometimes he managed to get out of it, but at other times he felt that a mysterious force was throbbing within and guiding him to tread along those dark passageways to explore something beyond this tangible world of existence.

On some of those mornings, waking early, he did nothing but paint pictures of a lonely wanderer walking along the path where he found no one, only darkness ahead, nothing more, nothing less. But as months passed, he began to ask himself: who was that mysterious force guiding him to walk on, even in the midst of that terrible darkness? Sometimes the answer came through the paintings he created in those days. Sometimes it came through the silence of his heart, through the stillness of those dark nights when, quite miraculously, he found himself aligned with the thought of who he was and from where he came.

You may be surprised and wonder how it is possible for one to align with such a thought while being completely alive and present with one's physical entity in this tangible world of existence. Though at first those questions frightened him greatly, one night the answer came in the form of that dream experience he shared with me. Quite surprisingly, he realised that descending further into those dark passageways, following the guidance of that mysterious force within, was nothing but probing deeper into the depths of his being, into the origin of his eternal existence, and finding a different meaning of his entity as well.

Darkness Is Nothing, but Allowing Your Inner Self to Be Introduced to the Truth, Within

Most of the time, we tend to relate darkness with something negative, totally ignoring the fact that darkness is not always to be considered as something evil, something to be scared of, but rather something mysterious to be explored in a newer way. And that dream experience of that painter was not an exception to that. It was not only a dream for him but a higher realisation; a realisation meant to remind him of one of the primordial dark nights from which he came into this world of existence and into which he will be merged. Probing deep into those dark passageways is not merely descending into them and losing yourself in their corridors of meaninglessness, wandering here and there and searching for your identity with a hopeless heart. Rather, it means to probe more deeply within and find that primordial secret code of your existence, deeply ingrained in that darkness.

Here, in this section, I would like to introduce you to another dimension of our existence, another reality of our entity that we so often tend to ignore. But it is already within us. Sometimes, we tend to avoid the darkness of our souls, considering it as something negative. We get scared of it. Sometimes, it leaves us awe-struck for a moment. But if we allow ourselves to descend more into the depths of that darkness, we can feel how much strength, how much power it already has. Yet we tend to ignore this fact and keep ourselves detached from that eternal source of energy, engaging ourselves in the search for our identity without knowing that the source of light, our own identity, cannot be perceived without delving deeper into this darkness within, as it is the ideal source of power and strength since the primordial time of our existence.

Here once again, I would like to remind you that the dream experience of that painter was nothing but a revelation, something like a mirror itself, where the darkness may not appear as something indistinct, frightening or monstrous, but as something very much reinforcing and creative, like a constructive force that would give him the strength to face the truth, the ground of his being and his eternal connection to the everlasting cosmic night. And herein lies its reality, its eternal enigma, to inspire us to probe more deeply into the depth of our being and reveal before us its primordial connection with our soul, with the greater womb of our existence, with eternity itself, reminding us once again that our existence is not to be reflected only in the light of day, but to be perceived even in the midst of terrible darkness. It introduces us to the depth of our being — the reality, the core of our existence—that is still within us, helping us to explore a different dimension of our being where, quite surprisingly, we can feel that we are already aligned with the eternal truth of our cosmic presence. And then we need not be baffled, we need not wander around in a hopeless manner; rather, truth will come as our only saviour, and once again we begin to perceive the reality of our spiritual existence.

While walking along the path where you may have no one but darkness as your only companion, never let yourself feel that you are lonely in this world. Rather, probe within, delve deeper into your entity. There, once again, you may stumble across that darkness, but at the same time, you must feel a murmuring voice of some enigmatic force inspiring you to move forward without a hitch. If possible, let us allow your consciousness to feel that voice. She is still lingering within your heart:

I know you are getting overwhelmed, my dear! But trust me, this is not the moment to be scared of, not the moment to be considered as something trivial, but something to be perceived if possible, try to feel me within your heart, within yourself, within your entire entity and I know you can feel me in your every presence, as I am not the darkness alone, but very much aligned with your true being, and will be with you forever, for you are not away from me but very much aligned with your true being, yes! I am that primordial energy from which you came and into which you will be merged, and it is in me you will find the secret code of your existence that is eternal and deeply connected to the divine source of universal intelligence.

Let's Probe More into the Dark and Feel the Mystery of Your Soul Once Again

Probing more into the dark is not only descending down but delving further within your own entity. And herein lies the mystery of those dark passageways, the mystery of your soul that apparently seems to appear as something unrecognisable, something to be scared of, but actually the origin of your spiritual existence; that absolute nothingness from which you mark your presence as something. And this is the magic of your existence, the magic of the universal creative intelligence.

In the previous section, I have already mentioned a dream experience of that painter. If you're thinking it was only a dream experience for him, let me assure you it was not such a simple one; rather, it was more like a quest than a dream, a quest for his identity, a search for his origin that he somehow lost in those labyrinthine tunnels of meaninglessness and existential crisis.

So, never be scared to encounter that darkness, as it is already within yourself. What you need to do is only to walk along those dark corridors without question, wherever it wishes to lead you. Rather, tread that path with strong belief in your heart and allow the mystery to unfold in a miraculous way. And trust me, dear, only there you can find that secret code you've been searching for a long time. Surrendering yourself to that darkness not only helps you realise how strong you are, but also brings serenity to your heart, making you realise that this darkness is the very core of your existence. It is actually that intangible, dark canvas of eternity that always holds the higher truth of our existence and always inspires us to paint something new upon it, which, in depth, is eternally connected to the universal source of creative intelligence. And trust me, this vast and dark canvas of eternity always allows your consciousness to probe deeper within and inspires you to feel that universal, eternal energy to which you belong, since the time of your presence and in your spiritual existence to come.

When darkness comes, roaring aloud, trying to engulf your entity
Yes, with a heart-rending sound, you may startle for once!
May ask for help, but finding no one coming forward
To make your ground, except that everlasting darkness
And darkness ahead.
Then never feel bad in your heart, my dear,
There must be some other truths to share,
Another reality that still speaks of your power,
But this time not a simpler one,
But of a higher strength within,
Out of which only divine energy can emerge,
To fill the void,
To fill your heart with wonder and awe once again!

Most of the time, we tend to consider this darkness as something evil, something that has to be eradicated without a hitch, and totally ignore another dimension of our existence, whereas it is undeniable that we cannot feel the presence of some graceful light without this darkness. In that sense, it is the ultimate reality of our spiritual existence. We are all searching for it, wishing for self-exploration, but at the same time becoming frightened of its monstrous, everlasting tentacles that spread all over our entities. We become scared of that, ask for help, forgetting that the help is to be discovered only within ourselves, within the darkness instead.

To explain the point more clearly, I would like to share an incident involving a person who used to visit one of my friend's consultation centres for an unusual problem. In one of his sessions, I learned that it was actually freedom he had been seeking. And when asked by my friend, "How do you think you would get that?" he replied very gently, "If I am able to keep myself in a dark room, it would be better for me to feel that freedom."

At first, his words startled me a lot! You may also wonder how it is possible for one to lock oneself in a dark room and yet feel a sense of freedom at heart. But herein lies the magic itself, the truth of one's self-exploration that helps him to stand before his own reflection, even in the midst of that darkness. Though most of us would consider that person merely a depressed soul who, in a fit of despair, chose to remain in a dark room, avoiding all circumstances and external activities but the real fact was not like that. That is why, instead of suggesting that he should come out of that dark room, my friend advised him to stay in that darkness as long as he wished for. According to him, that person was actually in search of his own identity and at that very moment was facing a dilemma within himself. His wish to remain in that dark room was nothing but an attempt to align with his primordial existence. Though it may seem unrealistic in this world of material reality but actually it holds the essence of reality itself, the reality of his being and his eternal existence. And the more he remained with that darkness, the more he would be able to align with the truth he already carried within — the truth of a mystery, the truth of his spiritual existence.

Bringing one out of that darkness and making him feel the grace of divine light may seem to us only as an overnight task, but the fact is not like that. Rather, it is a process of self-exploration where darkness is the only mirror through which to behold our reflection, that primordial reflection of our true being.

Here darkness not only comes as a mirror but also as a stage of our awakening, as a stage when, quite spontaneously, our consciousness inspires us to be with that darkness and to probe more within. Sometimes it is to have an ideal self-reflection, sometimes in order to emerge in a newer way towards a different direction where darkness is not to be seen as something destructive, but rather as a constructive force within, in order to erase all our disequilibrium, to ground our being, to make us feel once again that darkness is not to be feared, but something primordial as the cosmic night, to be embraced in order to be in close communion with our deeper self, from where we will be able to find our true home, the true ground of our being. And it would be more explicable if you pay some heed to the last few words uttered by him when he came to my friend's consultation centre for the last time:

"Yes! I chose to be in darkness. Somehow, in those days, I started to feel that I was genuinely myself. All the dilemmas I had been suffering from, quite miraculously, started to fade away, and the more I descended into that darkness, the more I felt I was aligning with my true essence, something primordial and eternal. Most of the time, I used to feel a longing for that darkness—the source of my being, the source of my existence as well. Your suggestions to spend some time alone in that darkness, in that solitude, did not divert me at all, but rather guided me to feel my true essence, the origin of my existence, once again.

It was a stage of a higher recognition, moreover, the stage of a reconciliation with that primordial, cosmic darkness that I already have within. And still now, I feel it was a stage of an awakening that inspired me to shed off all other dilemmas and directed me to emerge in a newer way, aligning truly with my roots, as that was the ideal time when I found the true candles of my existence within myself, even in the midst of that darkness.

Darkness is nothing but a gateway to enlighten yourself with the truth of your greater womb.

If you want to know yourself properly, in a way where the only spokesman is the depth of your soul, let me assure you that this darkness is the only guide to feeling that depth within. Without it, you will never be able to know your centre in a proper way. And most of the time, in search of our ideal centre, we delve more into the darkness within and sometimes lose ourselves in its mysterious dark chambers. But at the end of the day, quite surprisingly, we are introduced to the hidden core of our existence — that secret code of our entity in the midst of that darkness, even within the darkness of ourselves. The more we descend into its depths, the more we are introduced to the real power, the real strength of our existence. It is nothing but the doorway of coming back to your home once again, as it is the primordial source of our energy, an eternal power centre of our being.

Whenever we align ourselves with the deeper core of the darkness within, our ordinary consciousness automatically leads us towards a state of higher revelation and helps us to gain a different spiritual insight, enabling us to evolve in a newer way where darkness no longer seems something obscure or distressing, nor something that makes us feel distraught or injured, but rather as an eternal energy to be perceived within the depth of our being, where no one else but the soul resides. And in that way, it is that stage of our consciousness when we automatically become aligned with our cosmic presence, with our spiritual existence.

Recognising the true worth of our existence and aligning ourselves with that darkness within is not only the gateway to feel the ideal self-reflection but also the stage of our awakening when we begin to be enlightened in a different way. We start to feel our eternal presence more creatively. And from here begins the true recognition of our ideal home, of that greater womb from which we came and into which we will merge again, as we are nothing but spiritual beings in human form, eternally connected to the divine source of universal intelligence. Gradually, treading along those dark and secret passageways, quite miraculously, we begin to find our ideal centre within. Once again, that terrible darkness of silent nights starts to reveal to us a completely different picture of eternity, where we can truly feel what our life is and what our true purpose in reality might be.

In this connection, I would like to remind you all that going through the dark phases of our lives is nothing but preparing ourselves to endure inner pain and evolve our higher selves towards the direction where the dawn still waits for us, ready to embrace our souls once again for a higher purpose. So what we need to do is not blur our vision or frighten ourselves into feeling that we have no higher mission, but rather surrender our higher selves to the truth of that universal intelligence, so as to be enlightened to the true worth of our being. Aligning with the darkness within is not the end of our journey, but the beginning of an eternal sojourn that continually whispers into our ears:

Knowing yourself is nothing but being with the stillness you have within, and dancing with the spirit, with that darkness within, is actually reinforcing you to evolve in a newer way with all your primordial and spiritual essence.

In this connection, I cannot resist sharing with you a surprising experience that happened to me a few years back. I still remember that night when, in a miraculous way, I started to feel that my being was becoming aligned with the perfect stillness of that silent night. An inner voice was trying to mumble something, something inaudible yet deeply perceived within. It was like a deeper calling, a call of my soul, I felt, trying to merge with that dark night, with that eternal silence she bears within. From that very moment, I began to feel that I am nothing but a spiritual being, eternally aligned with the truth of that cosmic night, connected to the truth of the universe that is always inspiring us to evolve in a newer way towards the meaning of eternity.

The clouds in the sky, the perfect stillness, and the entire nocturnal beauty suddenly appeared before me as something very close and true to my being, since the primordial time of my existence. At that very moment, I felt that the perfect stillness of that night was nothing but the deeper core of my being, the reality of my existence in a cosmic sense. That night, I was very much with myself. My inner world was continually inspiring me to perceive that darkness within once again. That experience was not explicable in any tangible way, but something to be perceived, and that special feeling came to me that night in the form of poetry. Here I am sharing some excerpts from it:

It is like a motionless picture, standing still
With all its grace, all those dark patches bearing within
I was nothing but only a witness there, I felt
Something like a tattered cloth, like some broken pieces, I guessed
That nocturnal air was harking me back,
Somehow, I felt a greater truth calling me back
Once again to my root,
Perhaps, to paint another shade of reality
And to make me feel I am one with that darkness,
With that truth of eternity!

9 | Depression: A State of Self-Reflection

"Still, I don't know how it came to me, how that brooding, all-encapsulating sadness gradually started to cast a spell over my existence. That situation was completely beyond any consolation, and the meaningless existence that I was bearing with me only propelled my energy to choose the path of isolation and hopelessness. It was a painful journey indeed! It seemed that the entire stage of my existence was crumbling down, and I was totally unable to find the words to define myself, my situation altogether. It was not that sense of ennui or boredom I'm talking about, but rather a sense of helplessness that was ultimately engulfing my entire existence at that time. I still remember that in those days, I could do nothing but ruminate over those happy lullabies of my earlier days, when I used to drink life to the lees! Then, I didn't even realise where that hopeless journey was taking me. But I realised that my soul was crying aloud, and there was a higher need for me to help her out and to ground my being with her seed…"

She pauses for a while; tears roll down her cheeks;

"I don't know, how do I interpret it? But something happened, and quite miraculously, even during that painful journey, I was introduced to the higher purpose of my life…"

Most of the time, whenever we talk about the word *depression*, a sense of hopelessness quite automatically comes to mind. We start to consider this state of depression as nothing but the end of our existence. But here, at this juncture, I would like to remind you that the stage you are considering as the end of your life is nothing but a stage of self-reflection; a stage to rewind your journey once again and to move on with a renewed spirit and grace.

Unfortunately, most of the time we forget this truth and ultimately accept ourselves as some mere losers, mourning over past sorrows and regrets. But this was not the case for that drama artist. On the contrary, during that depressive state of hopelessness, she ultimately managed to free herself and inspired her inner self to speak in her own voice. The same stage she was scared of just a few days earlier finally proved to be the ultimate place of her soul's freedom. And herein lies the miracle; the miracle of moving on and emerging before the audience in a newer way, with greater spirit and a fresh mark.

Are You Depressed? Maybe You're Only at the Crossroad

On a superficial level, the word *depression* may bring along a sense of hopelessness, a never-ending journey from which escape seems utterly impossible. But if we probe deep into the matter with a compassionate heart, we may perceive that this depression is nothing but an existential crisis that a wounded soul suffers from. It is the crisis of deprivation, I feel, a yearning to be grounded in your soul's real essence. In that sense, this depressive stage is nothing but a crossroad to cover up. Maybe, it is a meeting point to reflect upon yourself in a greater mirror.

Instead of grieving over sorrows and regretting losses, this stage of depression may also be taken as a time to pause for a while, allowing yourself to perceive your soul's voice. In that sense, this stage may also be considered a new beginning. A stage where you may come with all such questions as, "Who are you?" or "Where do you come from?" And the moment you raise such questions, quite automatically, an existential crisis begins. But now it is completely your choice how to handle this situation. Is it a stage to mourn over past grief, or a stage to know yourself in a self-reflective manner?

The choice is yours. But trust me, all this excruciating pain and suffering that comes along with this state of depression is not to hold you back or belittle your existence. I feel this is divine protection itself, making you strong enough, reminding you of your spiritual existence, and especially preparing your soul to evolve in a newer way. And yes, herein lies the miracle itself!

In a deeper level, this stage is actually one of transformation, where a soul suffers greatly from agonising pain and continues to struggle internally. It is that state of utter incongruence when the soul is not anchored to its true sense of being, and the consequent result is nothing but a spell of hopelessness.

But remember, it is actually that crossroad where you need to pause for a while, to allow your inner self to be grounded in the truth of your existence. And trust me, you will definitely receive that divine protection your soul yearns for, even in that utter state of hopelessness.

In a deeper way of interpretation, this stage of depression is actually the stage of an abandoned soul who is continually struggling to be grounded in her true being, but, unfortunately, encounters failure each time. But remember, it is that very state where, quite unknowingly, you are gradually shedding off your old identity and preparing your inner self to evolve in a more self-reflective way. As a result, this transformation comes with divine protection, bringing you back to your soul's heritage and introducing your inner self to the true purpose of your life.

Depression: A Stage of Getting Introduced to Your Spiritual Existence

In a deeper sense, the depressive stage can be seen as a gateway to knowing yourself in a self-reflective way; a stage to behold yourself in a larger mirror and rediscover the hidden worth of your soul once again. It is that dark phase of your life that can lead you towards a meaningful realisation, enabling you to perceive your soul's choice in a deeper way. In an actual sense, this depression is nothing but the deep, agonising pain of a wounded soul who is trying to search for the meaning of her existence but continually failing to do so.

And mostly during this journey of failure, many souls suffer from the loss of being abandoned by their real selves. In that sense, depression does have a meaning indeed. In a way, I feel this state of depression is nothing but divine protection, meant to make you feel that you are strong enough to hold your existence; you are strong enough to create your own shelter with the help of your higher self, quite like that drama artist who, in spite of having lost the last hope of life, once again succeeded in coming out of that depressive state and allowed her soul to spread her wings in a newer way of survival. She did not choose to leave her performance; rather, she preferred to be on the stage with all her inner strength and renewed exuberance.

"Yes! It was that turning point of my life. A catastrophe indeed. A moment of reflection when life told me to pause for a while and ask myself, 'Is this the way I wish to lead my life? Is this how I wish to feel my existence?' And the moment these questions arose in my mind, quite unknowingly I started to become aware of my spiritual existence. All my old identities seemingly started to fade away, and once again, I started to feel that Nature was demanding something different from me. Yes! That was the moment of my rebirth! A moment of transformation, trans creation indeed!"

These were her last words when we met her for the final time in that hotel room in Chennai after a concert. I still remember her face, filled with contentment and satisfaction. It was not the satisfaction of victory, but the satisfaction of reconciling with her soul, I felt; a satisfaction akin to visiting her home after a long period of arduous struggle and bereavement.

This state of depression actually reveals to us the truth and reality of our existence, reminding us of that spiritual truth: the truth of our being and of our life as well. The more we confront the dark realities of our lives, the more we get to know where lies the hidden worth of our inner selves. We get to know that we are nothing but spiritual beings in human form. And I feel the more we encounter loss and grief, the more we may sense that there is a hidden truth always lurking within our entity, and that hidden truth is nothing but the truth of the soul itself; the truth that continually reminds us of our spiritual existence and, even in times of utter hopelessness, whispers into our ears:

Now it's time to move on, now it's time to see yourself in a newer way, and to transform and evolve your energy with a newer grace of enlightenment!

Let's Surrender Your Depressed Self to That Universal Power of Intelligence

During that state of depression, your ego may continually call you back, may break you down and impel you to ask yourself, "***Why me? Why me?***" It may also make you feel overwhelmed, and sometimes may even induce you to take fatal decisions. But trust me, dear, if you allow your ego to interpret this situation, you will definitely bring total chaos into your life. Instead of allowing your ego to resolve the matter, allow your soul to intervene. Yes, it is only your soul that has the power to lift you up and hold your hand once again for a new life to grow. And herein lies the magic—the magic of your spiritual existence, the magic of shedding your old identity and evolving with the rhythm of your soul's choice.

At this juncture, I would once again like to remind you that walking down the path of hopelessness and despair during this stage of depression may also be considered as a gateway to embark on a newer journey—a gateway to revisit your inner wisdom once again and to introduce yourself to the truth of life itself. And I feel this can only be possible if you surrender your higher self to the truth of that universal power of intelligence, for therein lies the magic—the magical power of your soul itself.

And I feel that the more you start to believe in this universal power of intelligence, the more you can perceive that your ordinary consciousness is gradually transcending towards that state of higher consciousness. And in that higher state of consciousness, quite automatically, you can feel that you are not lonely in this tough world of sustenance. Rather, you have that power inside you to grow according to the universal law of Nature itself.

In that sense, this state of depression is not one to mourn over past sorrows, but a state of reflection indeed, a state to sit face to face with your real self and ask, ***Is this the exact way you wish to lead your life?*** And I am sure you will definitely get your answer. But what you need to do is surrender your higher self to the truth of that universal power of intelligence. This complete surrender alone can bring change within your being. Even this surrender alone can help you to come out of that depressive state and realise that you, too, have the power within to stand your ground; you, too, have a gracious light within your being that can wipe out all the dark, pitchy clouds of hopelessness and despair.

And the moment you surrender yourself to that divine power instead of mourning over the loss, you will definitely feel that bliss within. This feeling cannot be defined in words, only perceived within. Then you will no longer be a wounded soul only to be humiliated, but a soul very close to that universal divine power of intelligence; a soul open to receiving the messages sent from that universal power of intelligence.

And herein lies the miracle! Herein lies the power of self-recognition, the power of having proper self-reflection in a newer mirror of enlightenment. And herein lies the true power of your soul itself!

10| Recognize Your Ego: Know Yourself, Perceive Your Soul Within

It was a voice inside,
I felt,
Roaring into my ears;
'It's no one, but only you and you
To make this change!
To shift the rudder,
To make your ground
With a marked shudder!'
I startled at once,
Didn't know what to say,
But only closed my eyes
And felt a 'difference'
From all those lies!
Felt within my entity,
With all the truth inside.
Then Eternity came
To embrace me once again,
To make me feel that
I'm nothing, but only
A divine essence!

In this materialistic world of continuous fulfilment and desires, when walking along the streets of frustrations, needs, and resentments, you may feel someone's voice inside your unconscious, continually tempting you to present yourself as someone superior before the world. Though at first, you may not recognise whose voice this is. You may even be lured by that tempting voice which continually provokes you to present yourself before the world as a total misfit, compared to your real self. And it is right from here that you start to misrepresent yourself before the world, sometimes to hide your real self knowingly or even unknowingly. As a result of this misrecognition of your real self, you quite automatically start to lose your connection with your centre within, and consequently become alienated from the outside world as well.

Do you want to know whose voice is this? What do you think? Is it really your own voice, or someone else's, or that of someone invisible whom you don't yet know? If you're fumbling a bit and cannot recognise the voice, let me assure you, my dear, that this is a voice coming from your unconscious. But you're quite ignorant of that. You feel it as your own voice, while it is not the voice of your real self but rather the voice of your ego, continually generating within you a desire for more. It also makes you feel that all the success you've achieved is based on your own power. Yet, in spite of all these self-aggrandising thoughts, you may still feel a lack within. Do you want to know what the cause of that lack is, in spite of having everything you own? The answer is, the lack you're feeling is not a lack of material needs, but a lack arising from your inner self, while, quite unknowingly, you're completely absorbed in your own ego.

Here, in this contemporaneous world, most of the time we tend to fall into the trap of our illusory ego selves, negating our true voice that comes from our soul, and consequently leading our consciousness towards a state of utter depression. Then, only to satisfy our ego, we don't even hesitate to harm others. Yet, aggrandising that ego of our unconscious is not life itself, but merely an elusive representation of a fabricated lifestyle, where we quite hopelessly choose to play upon the stage of falsity and illusion as masked players, inviting identity crises and meaninglessness into our existence, ultimately hindering the ideal path to feel our being in a spontaneous way and quite unknowingly forgetting the truth and beauty we hold within.

When the Ego Comes as an Illusion to Blur Your Thoughts in a Negative Way

Right at the beginning of this section, I would like to tell you that this ego, which, quite unknowingly to ourselves, continually influences our lives, is not always bad. Sometimes it also acts as a rejuvenating force, helping us to move forward in our lives, negating all kinds of dilemmas and dissatisfactions. In that sense, it also helps us build proper self-esteem, presenting ourselves before the world as socially bold people who can achieve anything despite the oddities and impediments we face on a regular basis.

But the problem is, it does not always happen. Most of the time, this ego tempts us to believe in an elusive reality that actually does not have any existence at all, but only channelizes our unconscious towards a state of having a false self-reflection, from where the sense of 'I'-ness becomes more important than perceiving our entity with all its truth and beauty. As a result of that, quite unknowingly to ourselves, we get entangled with a false, elusive identity that has nothing to do with our real selves. We start to believe that here on this earth, we need to present ourselves as superior to others, as someone with all the power in their hands, able to do anything to succeed, even at the cost of harming and degrading others, only to satisfy our ego.

But do you feel this is the ideal way to lead your life? Is this the ideal way to feel your being with all its true essence? If you are already seeking that answer, I would like to share with you the experience of an entrepreneur who was once successful but ultimately proved himself a failure only because he misrecognized his true self. Despite having everything in his life, he was never satisfied and always craved more, even at times complaining, disrespecting, and inflicting pain on others. In that course of aggrandising his ego above everything, quite unfortunately, he made himself a victim at the hands of his own ego. As a result, quite automatically, he started to lose his inner balance; his connection with his centre began to fade away, and it was only his ego that ultimately became dominant over his unconscious and finally managed to devour his entity in a shocking way.

You may be a bit surprised and think: was it the ego itself that was solely responsible for that failure, or were it his own thoughts that channelized his unconscious towards that totally different direction? If you are still wandering around this question, let me assure you that it was all because of that ego within his unconscious that prompted him to think that way, to be so self-centred that it ultimately brought about that fatal disaster in his life. And it was because of this ego-centred mentality that he not only lost his inner balance but also his business. All his employees ultimately turned against him. Even during those last hours of his misfortune, some of his employees heard him shouting at them, "It is not the company, but it's me for whom you all still belong! You all have your presence indeed!" He kept repeating those words again and again, even in the face of that total disaster, when there was no one to listen to his voice except his own ego, which ultimately proved itself as a detrimental force for him, bringing a total collapse to his entire kingdom and destructing his foundation as well.

The ego always channelizes your unconscious towards a totally different direction, keeping itself invisible from others, sometimes even keeping you unaware of its malicious effect. It not only blinds your vision but also generates within your survival self a sense of fear. This fear is not of anything unusual, but of sustaining in this world of survival; a fear of remaining superior to others. In this connection, I would like to tell you that this ego not only hinders you from seeing yourself reflectively but also prevents you from flourishing in your true essence. As a consequence of that, quite unknowingly to yourself, a superiority complex starts to develop within you, and once again, having no option, you surrender your entity to that frightening monster named Ego, depriving your soul's choice altogether.

It's Only the Awareness That Helps You to Feel Who You Truly Are in Reality

Do you want to know where the root cause of all this confusion lies? What was the root cause of that disaster that happened to that business merchant? It's all because of that illusory ego which, quite unknowingly, we indulge within ourselves, directing our consciousness towards a totally different direction from where we cannot perceive reality in its ideal essence. Instead, the reality itself starts to appear before us as elusive—a fabricated version without any real essence, leaving us wandering as hopeless survivors, seeking answers such as who we truly are and what our purpose on this earth is, yet never finding any clear answer. All the time, we get captivated by the enchanting charm of our I-ness and, again and again, become entangled in a complete misperception of our true identity.

In this connection, I would like to remind you that this I-ness is nothing but a construction of your ego, which, quite unknowingly, continually delves into your unconscious in an inconspicuous way. As a result, you can do nothing but pretend to play the role of a character who is starkly different from your real self. And herein lies the dilemma once again, along with that related existential crisis and meaninglessness of your identity as well. But the moment you start to recognise who you truly are in a real sense, you may feel that all this existential crisis will automatically begin to fade away, and quite surprisingly, you start to have a self-reflection from a much deeper perspective. This experience may differ from person to person. Some of you may think it is not the ego self whose voice is continually provoking you to present yourself in a totally different way, but the real you who is actually responsible for making you feel this way. But let me assure you, the fact is not like that.

As I feel, too much dwelling upon this extroverted lifestyle can only lead you to a distorted version of your own identity, where truth starts to appear before you as an illusion, and the falsified, fabricated life starts to appear as the truthful one. And herein lies the mastery of your ego that does not know your true worth and always tempts you to search for some external circumstances, while the truth always resides within yourself. But the more you get involved in those external affairs, the more you become alienated from the real core of your being and consequently get entangled with your fabricated egoistic self that actually has nothing to do with the ideal reality of your existence.

This fabricated self always has a tendency to feel superior to others. Never feel that your real self has that agenda. Your desire to become superior to others is not to be considered as a superiority complex, as I feel. Rather, it is an unconscious projection of your ego self that always feels insecure within, and as a result of that insecurity, it continually desires to be superior to others. It is not the desire of your real self but only that self-centred, image-making part of your unconscious that continually demands from others and tries to promote itself before the external world as the most powerful one, while the inner core of your being always wishes for something else. Yet as a result of its maliciously predominant power, gradually you may start to feel that you have no option but to be dominated by that powerful monster named Ego, and to feel yourself as the most powerful yet depressed one who has everything to dominate over, but nothing to be content with, nothing to feel the bliss within.

Most of the time, we tend to misinterpret this ego as our real self and fall into the trap of its malicious effects. Quite unconsciously, we misinterpret this ego self as the most powerful managing matron of our life and indulge ourselves to make our ground according to its whims through continually delving into our unconscious with some negative thought patterns, making ourselves feel that it is only the I (the self) who is responsible for all the happenings, for all the successful deeds, while actually being totally ignorant of the true power of our inner self. But the moment you become aware of the truth inside, quite miraculously, you start to feel the oneness within; you start to feel that you are, you have been, and you will be. Moreover, you begin to get aligned with your presence, with your true self, beyond that fabricated self which your ego used to present before the external world.

I feel it is not easy to completely alienate yourself from that ego self and to know your true identity in its essence, as this ego self is also connected to your survival self and sometimes helps you move forward in a constructive way. But most of the time, it tends to negate your real power and tempt you to present yourself to the world as someone very different from your ideal self. Yet the moment you become aware of who you really are and what true identity you have within, you start to feel an unexpected change not only in your thought process but also within yourself, resulting in a true emergence before this world of existence as your real self. And when this happens, quite automatically, those feelings of incongruence start to fade away, and once again, you begin to accept who you are in reality. You may start to feel that you are an entity far beyond that self-centred egoistic image-maker, far beyond the heraldic presence of that roaring voice drumming its existence every now and then.

Do you want to know what makes you feel this way? It is all because of an awareness that, quite unknowingly to yourself, has already started to grow within your entity, making you feel that you also have an identity beyond this external world, beyond this fabricated presentation of your illusory, egoistic self. And the more you align with that true self, the more you start to perceive the real core of your existence, the power of the absolute truth, and your connection with the power of eternity itself — the truth of your being, the truth of your existence as well.

So, whenever any negativity creeps around you, you need to be aware of the fact that the negativity is not within you. It is absolutely external, and you are only a silent observer of it. The moment this awareness starts to grow within you, you begin to realise that it is not your real self that is creating this negativity, but only your ego, which, through such malicious effects, creates such a nuisance. The moment you become aware of who you truly are, you start to feel that you are not only being liberated from that self-centred ego self and aligning with the real core of your being, but also evolving within and being introduced to the higher purpose of your life. And herein lies the magical power of transcendental consciousness — a consciousness that helps you to be conscious of your presence in a subjective way, rather than being conscious of any external objects.

Let Us Surrender Our Entity Completely to the Divine and Perceive Our Soul

In this contemporary world, when we are constantly immersed in material luxuries and always seeking something more, we often forget about ourselves. Here, I am not talking about that 'self' that is predominantly connected to our objective consciousness, but rather I am trying to help you perceive the inner self we all have within us since the primordial time of our existence, one we have never been introduced to.

In this section, I would like to remind you that mere objective consciousness cannot make you feel that special enigma within your entity. If you want to feel that special power within yourself, you need to be aware of who you truly are. And this awareness cannot come through mere objective consciousness, as it always distracts your mind with external matters that have nothing to do with your real self.

Trust me, that 'real you', that 'inner you', does not need any external appreciation, does not need to be categorised under the veil of any specific name, and does not need to be conditioned by the typical objective consciousness, but rather to be felt within—to perceive its stillness, its every presence, the unconditional, unveiled truth of its eternity. And herein lies the essence of your essential nature, your true being that only holds the truth—the truth of your soul, the truth of that divine essence that you have within you since eternity.

It is only with the help of this awareness that pure consciousness will quite automatically start to emanate from you—not only to evolve your soul in a newer way, not only to grow within once again, but also to mend that discord that once startled your entity, to awaken your being with that ideal truth of your existence that never asks you when or from where you came, but makes you feel that you are already content with everything. You had been, you are, and you will be with all your presence.

And herein lies the power of your pure consciousness, which helps you feel your cosmic presence and your true essence as a spiritual being. It helps you to feel beyond this tangible realm of earthly existence. At first, you may not see any difference, but if you probe deep within, you can feel where the true worth of this pure consciousness lies. Then you need not think about the span of time, nor bother about where you came from or where you will go, but you can feel your entire presence within and your connection to the truth of eternity.

Some of you may consider it a mystic experience; some of you may see it as something unreal, beyond this tangible frame of reality. But if you probe deeper within, you can feel that you are nothing, but only that pure consciousness beyond any form, beyond any time frame, an existence with all your spiritual essence. And the more you probe deep within your entity, the more you will be able to perceive that inner space that is absolutely beyond your tangible form and identity, beyond those materialistic needs and desires of your ego, beyond that fear that you are losing yourself.

At first, you may have the feeling that you are losing yourself, that you are not getting everything that can satisfy the so-called materialistic hunger of your conscious self. But if you probe further within your entity, you may quite automatically feel that you are getting aligned to that pure consciousness, in order to feel that perfect stillness within your being; moreover, with that formless and timeless dimension, with the truth of eternity, with that truth of universal divine intelligence. And the more you become acquainted with that truth of divinity within, the more you awaken to the true purpose of your existence, to that destined purpose that your soul wishes to have for her ideal emergence, for her true evolution.

That evolution not only helps you heal from all wounds and suffering, but also helps you emerge before the world with your true essence, and enables your inner experience to channelize your unconscious in a constructive way, in order to anchor your being in the right accord. Moreover, it allows you to be reunited with the ground of your being and to evolve once again, remaining true to your inner essence.

And herein lies the true magic of living your life with your true essence. The moment you start to feel this pure consciousness within yourself, you quite automatically begin to align with the truth of your inner essence. Then only can you feel that your life is not a fruitless existence, not something of mere survival clinging to your ego and materialistic desires, but something to be felt within, something to be beheld in a self-reflective manner.

To explore this point more deeply, I would like to share with you the personal experience of a lady who, through the help of an inner experience, ultimately managed to have a self-reflection that proved to be a revelation in itself; a revelation of her inner essence that she had within but had never felt before, even in her seventy-two years of life. In her own words, it was something truly beyond this tangible realm of understanding:

It was really a different experience for me; an experience to feel within, an experience to feel that inner space and to be aligned to that. At that moment, I was very much within myself! I was not even conscious of my surroundings, but very much conscious of the fact that I am. It was not the temporal me, throbbing within to emerge in a newer way, but the Inner Me who had been and would be, I felt. My physical body was breathing in itself, but I was not even conscious of that. You may think I was losing myself, but it was not like that. It was a special moment when my inner stillness appeared before me as a mirror itself, and all of a sudden, I was introduced to my real self. And the moment I was introduced to that real self, all the temporal dimensions dissolved at once, and I began to feel that I am nothing but an essence, the consciousness after all.

Yes, it was the consciousness that ultimately led her to feel the truth of her life, the truth of her existence as well. And that truth was far beyond her tangible existence, far beyond every material desire that, at every moment, had held her back.

Trust me, it is the consciousness indeed, through which you will once again align yourself with that highest truth, with that truth of divine intelligence. Once again, your soul will have the opportunity to open up to the truth of eternity. And once again, you will start to feel that you don't have any external world, but you are a spiritual one in a human form.

11 | Is The Devil Laughing? Let Your Divinity Smile Within

If no one holds your hand when life comes to you as a gigantic monster with all its habitual roar of laughter, shuddering your presence, making you feel frightened with all its scary tentacles and sniffing at you with sadistic pleasure, let me assure you, dear, that this is not the moment to be disheartened. Rather, this is the ideal hour to stand your ground; stand with all your strength within, and feel your presence with that everlasting grace that you always have on your face, called a "smile".

At first, you may startle a bit, may think how it's possible to make your ground while that scary monster is constantly knocking at your door and making you feel that you're nothing but a helpless creature struggling to survive in this world of existence. But if you probe deeper into this matter, quite gradually, you may start to feel that this devil is everywhere, possibly at every corner of our surroundings. Moreover, it is always trying to spread its tentacles with all its habitual, lustful glee — sometimes in an invisible way, sometimes with all its venomous tentacles in the names of envy, jealousy, anxiety, stress, betrayal and revenge, just to name a few. The list may be quite long, but here I don't feel much need to extend it further. Despite that devil within our unconscious, we also have our security code, called "smile", always lurking on our faces — not only to bring that signature mark to our expression but also to make us feel that we possess a special power within, not merely to sustain but to live with all our zeal and eternal fragrance.

Devil Is No One, But the Projection of Your Own Unconscious

In this section, I would like to tell you that this devil you're scared of is no one, and it cannot do you any harm without your consent. But the more you become involved in thoughts of negativity, the more you will welcome this devil, and the more it will spread its venomous tentacles towards your existence, frightening you, making you feel unnerved, and ultimately leading you towards a state of hopelessness and despair from which survival may seem a fruitless existence. But the fact is not like that; it is something else, something that cannot be explained tangibly, something to be perceived within, through the deeper core of your existence.

Our life is not a silver platter that glitters all the time, but something to be experienced and learned from. Yet most of the time, we tend to forget this fact and allow ourselves to be lulled by all the external glitter, completely forgetting our inner power and once again falling into the trap of noisy illusions. Through this process, quite automatically, we ourselves welcome that devil into our own territory, indulging it further and allowing it to take us into its grip, while actually it is nothing but an external force to lure us in several tempting ways. The more we become involved in those external illusions, the closer that devil comes to us. Gradually, we begin to feel that we are no one but helpless creatures, continually struggling in our lives and becoming mere tools in their hands.

To explain the point more deeply, I would like to share with you an incident that happened to a successful business owner who ultimately sabotaged the success he had gained throughout his lifetime. It was all because of the devil within his unconscious that demotivated all his efforts and perseverance, making him feel that he was not worthy enough to deserve any of it.

Actually, it started much earlier, especially during his childhood, when he was constantly humiliated by his surroundings. Even his own parents considered him hopeless; someone not meant to succeed, but only to lead a life of fruitless survival. Years passed, circumstances changed, and ultimately life proved to him not as a curse but as a miracle, a blessing in itself. It made him one of the most successful entrepreneurs in his surroundings.

But in spite of this massive change, something remained the same; that unchangeable thing was nothing but the devil within his unconscious, which ultimately proved itself a detrimental force, bringing his failure altogether. You may be surprised, may wonder how it is possible for anyone to feel unsuccessful while standing at the top of the success meter. But at this juncture, I would like to remind you that it's possible if you constantly allow that devil to spread its poisonous tentacles within yourself. And this case was no exception. If you go through his own words, you will easily comprehend the same:

"I didn't know what exactly happened that time, but somehow I used to feel that something was not happening right, and I must stay away from all this success, from all the prosperity that I'd achieved throughout my life. Sometimes I used to hear a hoary voice whispering into my ears, trying to make me feel that I wasn't worthy enough to deserve all this success. Everyone was envying me, sniffing at me, and I was there only to be humiliated and mocked by others!"

These were his realisations when he was already at the top of his success. You may be surprised; you may wonder why he was behaving in such an unusual way. And at this point, my answer is that these words were not his own, but of the devil itself that had found a permanent shelter within his unconscious in an inconspicuous way. Do you want to know what that devil was all about? It was nothing but his own negative thoughts, already ingrained into his unconscious from childhood through some traumatic experiences, which were still spreading their tentacles and tempting him to believe that he was nothing but a puppet at the hands of that devil itself. And that stern belief, though negative indeed, ultimately made him utter:

"It's all nonsense, the success and all that I've achieved. I'm nothing, absolutely nothing, and it is only failure and despair that I deserve to have in my life."

Here, my point is that this external society and its circumstances cannot be changed. We cannot take up the responsibility to change everything forever. But we still have that power within to make a change in our thought process, not only to crush the devilish laughter by the power of our soul, but also to bring back that divine smile within, in order to feel the true essence of our being in a deeper way; in order to feel that we're nothing but spiritual beings, eternal and powerful with all our primordial essence. And trust me, the moment you start to feel that divine smile lurking on your face, the moment you start to believe in yourself, you quite surprisingly begin to get aligned once again with your primordial essence that continually inspires and guides you to move forward in life, in spite of all external oddities and upheavals.

And herein lies the truth of your life, your spiritual existence as well, which has the power to make you smile in a blissful way and to fade away that devilish laughter forever. But quite unfortunately, it didn't happen to that entrepreneur, and ultimately, he chose to lead a life of despair in a solitary destination of his own until another miracle happened to him, and he was introduced to the true worth of his real self within, quite surprisingly.

Find Out Your Inner Truth and Encounter That Devil with All the Smiles You Have Within

Here, I would like to remind you a simple fact of our existence: we all have a divine and a devil self already ingrained within our unconscious. But it's always up to you which one you prefer to choose, because therein lies the real truth of our existence. Yet finding that divinity within is not an easy process to comprehend, but a reflection indeed to perceive; a reflection, a self-exploration in essence. And the case of that entrepreneur was not an exception. The devil of his unconscious had completely devoured his entity until he got reconnected once again with the eternal divinity within. And herein lies the magic of that divine smile, the magic of exploring yourself through the rays of that divine light. It was that divine light that ultimately helped him return to his centre and made him realise where the true worth of his being actually lay. And quite unknowingly, he came to know the real power of that divine smile that he had within since the primordial time of his existence, though he had never realised it before this ultimate awakening.

In this connection, I would like to remind you that the more you allow that devil to spread its tentacles by harbouring negative thoughts about yourself, the more distant you will become from your soul's choice. That devil can only lead you towards a state of meaninglessness. But if you pay heed to your soul's voice, you'll realise that reality does not lie in those negativities but in something else, something that may not be interpreted in a tangible sense, but must be perceived within, perceived with all your depth. And the moment you start to perceive your true self, your divinity within, you begin to align with the real truth of eternity itself.

And herein lies the importance of turning inward, descending into the depths of your unconscious and finding the divine self that has the power to crush the devil inside your being. The devil is nothing but an unconscious projection of our mind that doesn't match the real core of our existence, as we are connected to the universal source of divine energy since eternity. And herein lies the true core, the real worth of our existence. The moment we become aware of that divine source of energy residing within us, quite unknowingly, we start to feel the devil within fading away, and a new light of divinity merging with our being. Remember, it is the source of that divine smile within; it is the source of life itself—our guiding principle to channelize our consciousness towards a higher realm, in the right order, to restore our balance and perceive our divinity within.

In this connection, I would like to tell you that if you wish to feel that divinity within, you need to descend more into your depth, into the depth of your soul, wherein lies eternity itself. Keeping aside all our rational thoughts and interpretations, if you descend more into that depth within, you will be introduced to a different reality of our existence that is solely associated with your true self. And as I feel, if you are able to explore yourself into the deeper layer of your psyche, you would easily be one of the happiest souls in this world of existence. And this is the ultimate way, I feel, to perceive the serenity of divine bliss within.

It was really a magical moment when that entrepreneur got aligned with his true self and realised that his projection of that devil inside and all his frightful resolve were nothing but a separation from his ideal reality, which he himself also confessed as "a moment of mirroring myself"; a moment when his consciousness became totally aligned with that divine power of intelligence. Once again, he started to feel wherein lies the essential core of his spiritual existence. And the moment he started to realise this fact, quite automatically, a smile came to his face as a divine grace. He started to feel that infinite power within his depths. And once again, he began to perceive that his soul's voice had something special to make him believe that he also had a different purpose on this earth, and that purpose had nothing to do with that devil's laughter, but rather a purpose to believe in his soul's power, to feel his presence not only as a human being but as a spiritual being instead. And the moment he started to get that true reflection of himself, quite unknowingly, his pure consciousness began to speak with his depth, and all the disequilibrium created by that devil inside quite automatically started to fade away, and ultimately, his being found the ideal way to emerge before the world with all its spontaneity once again.

And herein lies the real power of our true being, the reality of our existence that need not be scared of that devil when it comes with all its malicious and harmful efforts, but what we need to do is only to light the candles of our faith deeper within our being and allow our soul to fly with all its divine essence.

Let's Surrender to the Infinite and Feel the Eternal Bliss Within

Feeling the divinity within is not only to contemplate and perceive the deeper meaning of your existence, but also to feel your eternal connection to the ultimate source of universal intelligence and to surrender your entity without any hesitation. It is that universal source of intelligence that continually guides you to move forward, negating all the vibes that the devil inside your unconscious tries to spread with its venomous tentacles. Your frightful resolve, your negative thinking, your depressing thoughts, or even your thoughts regarding jealousy, greed or sometimes the urge to take revenge on others are nothing but projections of that devil of your unconscious who quite inconspicuously tries to let you down and sometimes even lures you to stay in a dark dungeon of fruitless survival, perhaps to make you feel that you are nothing but a hopeless creature to be played by the whims of that devil.

And trust me, this happens only when you get separated from your spiritual centre. This separation not only hinders your soul from evolving once again but also channelizes your consciousness towards a totally opposite direction, quite contrary to the ideal choice of your true self. As this is the eternal force guiding you since the primordial time of your existence, any separation from that may hinder you from feeling the ultimate divine purity of your soul. What you need to do is only to surrender to that divine source of universal intelligence, to see within and feel that everlasting glory inside your entity.

That special connection will not leave you astray, but rather help you believe in your strength once again and make you feel that you are not alone on this earth, but already connected to a special energy that helps you feel your presence all day and night.

And herein lies the magic itself, the magic of your existence and the reality of your true connection to that divine force within. But the problem is that if we continually indulge that devil in our unconscious, remember, we are doing nothing but getting separated from our divinity within that we have had since the primordial time of our existence. Knowing yourself and surrendering your entity to that infinite truth of divine intelligence not only helps you to transcend your soul to that truth of eternity but also rejuvenates her to seek the real meaning of your existence; a meaning that is beyond this tangible realm of logical interpretations, a meaning that is inexplicable in a rational way but to be perceived within only through a blissful experience. And at that very moment, you start to feel that your pure consciousness is getting aligned with a higher wisdom, a wisdom of peace and serenity; a wisdom that never makes you feel your existence as a fruitless survival, running after some illusions and getting scared of several devilish encounters, but an existence instead where truth and beauty hold each other's hands in a blissful accord. Though intangible perhaps, it finds a tangible frame on your face, named "Smile", a divine smile instead.

If the night comes to you as a lonely castle
With a devil inside it, making you feel unnerved,
Never ever try to flee from that,
Never try to find the moon over the sky,
Rather, try to feel your presence within,
Like those stars overhead, dazzling bright
Feel that enigmatic hour and allow your heart to smile again,
Reminding yourself that you have nothing more to lose, nothing to gain

again,
But only to live, to breathe in your divine presence,
And to feel your soul's voice.
She is still humming within,
Smiling with eternity,
With all her magical essence!

12 | Deepen Your Faith and Feel the Magic

Whenever along the dusty road of your survival, the paltry self of your existence may ask you with an empty look, "How long would you have to continue this journey, as the darker sides of realities are continually knocking at your doorsteps?" you may think twice. Your depressed self may stumble over some nonsensical ramblings, being unable to find the answer your entity has been yearning for a long time. But I would suggest here that you never feel gloomy. Rather, at that very moment, try to probe deep into your heart. There, you may perceive the enigmatic presence of an energy, helping you to move forward.

The vastness of the sky may make you feel that there is a greater truth beyond this tangible world of mundane reality; the truth with the help of which the stars are still shining in their beauty, in spite of the darkness around them. You may be overwhelmed at first. But if you stand beneath that starry sky, glancing over it, you may feel that your entity is trying to tell you that your existence has a greater significance on this planet. And at that very moment, you may feel a gentle voice coming from the depths of your being:

"Life is not a mere survival, my dear, but an eternal journey to perceive, to make you feel that all the upheavals coming on your way are nothing but some blessings in disguise. Fathom deep into your heart, feel my presence. There, you may not find a dazzling fairy standing with her magic stick, but the presence of some divine magic who can

paint your fiery imagination on the frame of reality, making you believe that you have a special power within, and now it is the time to allow those miracles to happen.

You may be bewildered for a moment. Who is that special energy talking to you in such a gentle way? Your dwindling self may once again wish to stand under the starry sky, overwhelmed a bit. Then all the answers may also come quite in a surprising way, only to make you feel that they are coming from nowhere but from that inner seed where faith resides.

Here in this chapter, I would like to lay bare that eternal truth of faith and how it works from the innermost corner of your being, only to make you feel that your life is nothing but a blessed encounter of your soul with the divine.

When Faith Allows Your Unconscious to Search for a Higher Truth

Those of you who are thinking that faith is something external to be incorporated into your mind in order to see the magic, let me assure you that faith is nothing but that special power very much integrated within your being since the primordial time of existence. But you never listened to her higher calling and indulged yourself in a meaningless existence, from which life can only be viewed as a never-ending pursuit of something unattainable. Though in this age of turmoil, being faithful — or having faith in something or someone — may appear to you only as a textbook cliché. But if you are faithful even at the moment of any existential crisis you are going through, you may perceive where lies the mystery of that hidden truth. And that truth is nothing but to be self-reliant and allow the divine order to take hold of your circumstances, allowing your soul to be rejuvenated once again in order to feel the eternal grace of life.

A deeper faith helps you change yourself, bringing peace and harmony, aligning you with your soul's purpose, and leaving behind the old shell your ego once suggested you put on. Moreover, it enables your heart to move beyond, to pick up the broken pieces, so you can see life not as something unrealistic to encounter but rather something as another blissful encounter with your soul—a special purpose to attain.

It may also inspire you to imagine in a newer way, leading your consciousness to believe in an unseen reality beyond this tangible world, where your soul can have the chance to encounter something divine and magical. Despite living in this mundane world of reality, it always inspires you to believe in another dimension where self-integration grounds you for your destined purpose, allowing you to feel eternity within a moment. This way of grounding your being in your true purpose leads your unconscious to that state of ultra-motivation from which you can create something out of nothing.

Whenever your stumbling feet pause for a moment and need to take some rest for a while, faith may come forward from the innermost depth of your being to nourish your soul, to console your being with her loving message:

Your journey has not finished yet, my dear. Let us try to descend more into the depths and feel the presence of those shimmering flames, burning still at the end of that darkest tunnel. You may be astonished. But never feel alone. Let us try to feel the truth, the truth of those shimmering flames still burning to soothe your wounds, your scars to mend. Maybe there you will find the eternal truth of your existence, the truth of believing your destiny once again, surrendering your entity completely to that eternal divine intelligence.

Discover a True Believer within Yourself

Whenever, during any moment of existential crisis, the shadowy part of your entity harkens you back, indulging you to fall into the trap of despair and dissatisfaction and beguiling you to think that faith is nothing but an elusive way of consoling yourself and, in this world of mundane reality, it has nothing to do with building your foundation, try to remember that faith is not something elusive, but rather an eternal energy that helps you grow both psychologically and spiritually. Losing faith in yourself is not only losing hope in your existence but also negating that spiritual centre, the ground of your being. So, whenever you are becoming faithless, try to remember that you are cutting that eternal cord, that secret code of your entity, resulting in a form of depression and existential dilemma.

As I feel, being faithful or having faith in a divine order of the universe not only introduces before you a different state of your being, but also that self-revelation comes as a transformative energy along with the emergence of a newer you. And this newer version knows no boundaries of fears and restraints, but only allows your being to be motivated, to embrace that eternal grace, that grace of continuity, that grace of accepting life as it comes, even at the moment when your fearful energy shrieks in terror and says:

"There is a dark night ahead!
No one is visible in the outer alley,
I don't know, where I need to go?
Is it there, I left my last show?"

This newer version never indulges you to feel your life as a mere show, but always leads your ordinary consciousness towards that dimension of a higher consciousness from where you may not identify yourself as a separate being wandering over the earth to act, but rather as a being in perfect unison with the eternal force of the universe only to attain that higher calling that your soul has been yearning for since primordial time.

Though some of you may interpret this feeling as a mystical experience to encounter, I feel, here begins the birth of a true believer who can accept this experience not as a temporary reclusion of his or her mind, but as a permanent ascension of his or her soul towards the realm of continuity, towards the state of being in perfect harmony with the soul's eternal abode.

When Faith Helps You to Revisit Your True Home, Once Again

When darkness crawls across the valley,
Allowing no one to come forward-
The crescent moon smiles a bit,
Perhaps to make you feel;
There is some other way around
Let's probe, more into the deep!
You may find, faith is coming along
With her gentle, silent steps,
Only to show you the home, make you feel-
You've, some special significance!

Here lies the truth, the harmony of our existence, that never allows us to fall into deep despair, but quite unknowingly allows faith to come forward from the deepest corner of our heart like that crescent moon, reminding us once again that we still have some special purpose on this planet. Faith not only heals us but also helps us to bring back our strength with that eternal grace, aligning us to our true spiritual centre. It enables us to see the ordinary things through an extraordinary perception, allowing our soul to be free from any restraint, not to meet any temporary achievement, but to live our destiny along with the celebration of this life, along with the spark of eternity.

In this connection, I would like to share with you an incident of a business owner who, in spite of his utter failure, never allowed his heart to indulge in any negative thought pattern, but always had a stern belief that someday something miraculous would happen in order to bring back that light of hope into his life. I still remember those words that he said during my last visit to him at one of the cafeterias in New Delhi:

"I failed in every respect. My business had totally collapsed. Those sleepless nights are still vivid in my memory. But I never lost hope, never allowed my heart to lose faith in the divine power. During those days, I had a strong belief in my heart that there was something special

for me, designed by the universe. And this failure is nothing but a blessing in disguise. And trust me, I was not wrong. That miracle actually happened. That night, there was absolute silence. The sky was almost clear. The stars were shining. Somehow, I felt they were not only shining but at the same time trying to align my entity with some higher truth. The crescent moon above was gleaming with her gentle beauty. I do not know how, but suddenly a deeper realisation I had. Perhaps it was trying to open me up. Somehow, I felt that as my homecoming, the deeper yearning of my soul to realign herself with her sweet home. My passion sparked, emotions mingled once again, probably to keep my spirit up. A new creation was just on the horizon, I felt somehow. There was something special. The perfect stillness of that night, the gentle beauty of that crescent moon, were enough for me to contemplate what faith is and how it may come into my heart space. Suddenly, I felt a perfect union of my soul with that divine intelligence governing the universe. I was encouraged by the thought that the next morning, something miraculous was going to happen. I went to sleep that night, praying only to the divine. And, quite surprisingly, I was not wrong. That miracle actually happened. An email was sent by one of my old investors, who was still interested in investing a large amount of money in my business, not only for the professional bond we once had, but also to help me out of that situation. I was very elated by that news. Tears came into my eyes, perhaps to thank that divine energy that had been with me that night. And the rest is history."

Let's Believe and Pray, Miracles Are on Their Way

Always remember that a faithful heart can create magic. Being faithful not only opens up the possibility of contemplating beyond the present circumstances, but also allows your soul to flow in a natural, spontaneous way to feel that grace of independence, that grace of an eternal truth. It always acts as an inner flame, silently radiating her energy in an invisible way, channelizing your unconscious towards a different, constructive realisation of accepting those realities where the circumstances may not be changed, but you may have that higher vision to change yourself according to a divine order.

Here, imagination plays a big role. Certainly, the imagination that has a positive direction helps you to believe in miracles. These kinds of imaginations always inspire you to believe that whatever you are dwelling on or aiming for has already been accomplished. Though some of you may consider it unrealistic, I would tell you that this method of believing something with a thankful and faithful heart has magic in itself. And here reality may not appear before you as a catastrophic experience, but rather as a sudden shift to recognise your inner power, to experience some spiritual encounters. Here, at this stage, faith comes as your only saviour to expand your consciousness to that level from where the word 'impossible' may appear as nothing but something very much elusive and indistinct.

It always fills your entity with transformative energy, investing you with a deeper sense of realisation, where passion and emotion blend to form a higher version of reality. It fills your heart with a divine magic, enabling you to feel blessed even when your survival self, in despair, asks, "Is it worth waiting when life itself appears as some mere waste?" Your faithful heart may come forward, assuring you, "Yes! It has been worth waiting! You still have that power within. Now, it is only a time to pray!"

A faithful heart never prays like a beggar, but prays with that inexhaustible power from his or her heart that always inspires you to look forward, to look Godward, not to look towards your problems, worries and fears. Always try to remember that becoming a true believer is another way of becoming a true survivor who does not survive as a wounded warrior, but rather survives with all his strength, completely surrendering his life to God. As I feel, prayer always acts as a bridge between your higher self and that divine intelligence surrounding the universe. So, always try to ground yourself, pray to the divine and ask for help. A heartfelt prayer never remains unanswered. And herein lies the divine magic, the magic of being a true believer!

A thousand times I prayed,
To bring that breakthrough
To give my life that long awaited shade!
But answers never came.
Only an energy, brimming within, I felt
I startled at once, asked myself;
"Who is that energy,
Guiding me, at this edge?"
Then an answer came
"I am your Faith, that shimmering flame,
Here I am to lift you up,
This time to your divine self.
To make you feel miracles are not far away
But just on their way;
The eastern horizon is glowing red
And now it is time
Only to
Pray, pray and pray!"

13 | Evolve Your Soul in a Creative Way and Heal Yourself

When reality becomes unbearable and you have no option but to move beyond, try to remember one thing: that your secret self, where your imagination resides, has always had a special plan for you. She will never let you feel alone; rather, she will always inspire you to move beyond this tangible world of mechanical reality and allow your being to embrace that higher truth, not to enjoy any momentary recluse but to evolve yourself, true to your existence, true to that creative spark of nature that your soul has been longing for since eternity.

In this connection, I would like to share with you a poem I once wrote in a trance-like state as I was searching for some unresolved answers. On that night, something happened out of the world and, quite unexpectedly, this poem came into my mind like a sudden flash of lightning.

I was still in that trance-like state, but an unknown muse kept guiding me deeper into my depths and helping me create those words, may be to find the answers to those unresolved conflicts I had been searching for a long time. Those expressions were like:

A total darkness it was
As He descended down into the depths,
There were still no valleys, no meadows to shape

There was nothing to be found, no one to sound
Only a void where one may wander around
But a sudden spark comes in His mind
Letting His heart speak again,
To spring up with a newer shine
The sky was still alone as a clean slate
But He paints some clouds on her,
Letting her shine again
To shine with all her favourite mates,
He lights up the stars at once, just to bring some colours
This time the fresher ones
On that immortal frame
To make her feel the divinity she always longed for
Since the time she came, since the time eternity came
With all its magic, all its grace!

When Imagination Sparks, Creativity Blazes Itself Out of Nothing

Do you want to know where that imagination came from that night? Here in this section, I would like to invite you into that world of unseen reality. It is that state of your mind that cannot be defined in any logical sense of linearity. It is not that energy that you may have in a tangible sense. But all of a sudden, you may feel that, out of nowhere and quite miraculously, it may lead you towards another dimension of reality that has a mysterious power of imagining something out of the box and creating something greater that you have never experienced in this mundane world.

It also helps you to descend into the depths of your being, where you may find nothing but some dark mazes to confront. You may be overwhelmed at first, finding no passageways to discover yourself, to have that reflection. But herein lies the depth, the value of your imagination that may help you to expand your consciousness to that state of transcendental perception from where life cannot be viewed as an ordinary experience to confront, rather as an extraordinary existence, inspiring your artistic self to create a wonder out of a full void, out of a total darkness where once you got stuck for a long period of time. Then, suddenly, that mysterious force inside stirs you for once and pushes you forward to light some candles of your imagination on the canvas of that total void. Then you may feel that you have nothing to do but to surrender yourself to that mysterious force and dedicate your being to the creation of something new.

And when this happens, you may find nothing but the creation of a wonderful art as a blessed outcome that your soul may feel. As the very nature of your soul is creative and she moves beyond any constraints of tangibility, she also allows the gift of your imagination to embark on a newer journey in order to enter into the new world of infinite possibilities, where creativity is not something to enjoy for a momentary recluse but something to evolve yourself in a newer way. And then eternity will speak the last word for your creation and for your existence as well.

When Creative Imagination Serves to Inspire and Recreate Your Destiny

You may feel that this gift of creative imagination is only applicable to those who are artistic in nature or have the capacity to see the world in a different way. In that sense, this is for those who are poets, artists or those who are spiritually gifted. Though you are right to some extent, as they really are that special, I personally believe.

But at the same time, you may be surprised to learn that we all possess within us this inherent quality of creation, but never allow ourselves to peep inside. This imagination not only helps you break free from traditional, linear thought patterns but also allows your consciousness to flow naturally, so you can be who you truly are. And in the course of this emergence with all your newer colours, you can feel a more mature sense of growth within, a growth that always prompts you to evolve even in the midst of any crisis that you are experiencing. It always leads you to believe in an unseen world of reality, yet at the same time brings you back to your true self in a more constructive way for creating something new, for moulding a newer shape on that sculpture that once your artistic energy had aspired to create.

To explain it in a lighter way, I would like to share a personal experience I heard from one of my psychologist friends. He loved to work with his clients in a very creative way, laying bare their insights and helping them heal in a self-cognitive way, with the assistance of their souls, in a natural way of creating something new that their soul asked them to create. During the course of his treatment, quite unknowingly, the patients start to believe that they themselves are the healers and the artists of their own life. And during that course, they also have in their minds that this task of engaging their depth in creative work is not only helping them to heal themselves but also encouraging them to create something extraordinary, very much aligned with their soul and at the same time providing them with an opportunity to reconcile with their true self that their destiny always yearns for.

When Your Soul Finds Eternal Solace through Creative Art

As we all know, the soul is not something to be touched but something to be felt within. And that is why she never understands any linear or logical form of language, rather always prefers to present herself in a non-linear, symbolic manner, where you may not get puzzled yourself but find a deeper truth, a different dimension of reality, and your existence as well. And here comes the advocacy of art itself that, in its beauty of exploring a higher truth, always speaks for nurturing your soul in a newer way, in a way when time pauses for a while and you yourself are not aware of who you are and what you are doing at that very moment, but simply allow yourself to feel its magic. Art is not something that comes from that logical, exterior part of your conscious self, but rather comes from the innermost depth of your soul, which knows no boundaries, knows no language and for whom images and symbols are the only talking personas to converse with.

In most of the moments of artistic creation, you may feel that you are surrendering your inner self to a mysterious divine energy that continually inspires your consciousness to reach towards a special dimension where eternal serenity awaits you, making you feel that your existence has a special meaning.

Here in this section, I would like to share another mysterious gift that our soul has within her; this is the gift of healing herself. Whenever she feels trapped inside a dark dungeon of isolation and existential despair, it is her very nature that inspires her to release all the past burdens. But she cannot do it in a tangible sense of reality. And here at this juncture, creative art comes forward as her only saviour and sweeps her off her feet towards a magical world where she can create and evolve herself once again, beyond this mundane world of reality, in order to celebrate life with a deeper feeling that has always been needed to heal herself, to be aligned with her creative potentials, to be with her eternal presence, even in the face of distraught and disequilibrium.

As the earth seems to collapse
And darkness engulfs your tiny presence
Never feel distraught for a while,
Never feel gloomed again!
Just stare at the sky, instead;
There you may also have
Another sight of an earthly heaven
Calling you back to create yourself
But, this time, on a newer canvas
On a newer frame!

Creative Imagination Provides a Different Insight for a Higher Revelation

Creative imagination does not serve the purpose of creating something new only; rather, it creates a different dimension where your soul can converse with you in an ineffable yet intuitively perceptible way. Then you may not be considered as an artist in a literal sense but may be considered an artist of your life, an artist of your own being, where through the process of inner cognition you are not only emerging your presence in a newer form before the world but presenting the art of your life as your own creation, very much true to your soul's purpose. And sometimes true to that dimension of your existence where your destiny always waits to help you in order to shed off your external shell, to bring you back to your true purpose where your heart resides in order to evolve within, not only to shape your sculpture in a newer grace but by recreating your life once again as a true sculptor and to celebrate the true meaning of life itself.

In this connection, I would like to share with you an extraordinary incident of a lady that I heard from my psychologist friend. It was a miraculous incident of a simple woman who, quite unexpectedly, decided to be an artist, leaving behind her old career as a banker, simply on an overnight decision. If you go through her reminiscences, you will understand that it was not an overnight decision that readily came into her mind and made her a poet. Here, I would like to bring before you some of her thoughts that she shared with my friend during the days of her consultations. Somehow, she had gone through some traumatic experiences, not only in her working field but also in her personal life, as I got to know from my friend. And it was the identity crisis that made her consult a psychologist, and quite miraculously, she found her identity restored in its ideal form in a way of her own creation, where her insight revealed the higher truth of revelation. You must be eager enough to know what had happened that helped her to get back to her real self. I would like to share that experience in her own words, as I heard from my friend:

At first, when I started writing according to your suggestions, it felt like a complete void to me; I felt it was utterly impossible to ruminate over past experiences and write about those incidents in a logical way. At the same time, it was troublesome for me to look forward and leave behind all those pains that I had already gone through. At that time, poetry was never my cup of tea. But you suggested to write down, if not in a poetic way, then with the help of symbols and images. I tried to do that during those initial stages, but I found no words. During the first few days, I used to write some gibberish, sometimes simply allowed my heart to talk with me in some forms of painting. The first painting I pictured was the painting of darkness, where nothing can be figured out. Days passed by as silence stepped in, and in a more intuitive way, I started to feel some mysterious energy continually throbbing within to express something. Quite unknowingly of myself, I took my pen and paper and wrote my first words on that blessed night:

"As the silence steps in,
The nocturnal air seems to hover around,
Harking me back, to where?
The stars may know, but I do not.
Maybe towards that way
Where someone is waiting for me,
To bridge a gap that once I made
In the course of this earthly cacophony!"

On that night, for the first time, I felt the presence of something special within me, the presence of something that is beyond this tangible world of reality. It came in an unexpected way. At that very moment, I was not in me, but I felt someone else was writing that write up on my behalf. I only surrendered to her, and she wrote those words. The next morning, when I shared this experience with you, you only smiled and assured me that it was not me but my intuitive artist who took that pen and paper on my behalf.

But after some days, in an unexpected manner, she went away, leaving me once again as a barren island. I did not find any words to console me. On those nights, I could not sleep properly. I used to walk along some solitary beaches, sometimes through the labyrinthine passageways around the hilly roads. But in vain, she was nowhere. That made me cry! Made me to kneel before the vast expansion.

Some days later, I could feel her once again. She came to me as a starry sky, under which I once again began to feel my presence, not in my human form but in an intangible form, beyond this world of mundane reality, something very much attuned to the energy of the universe.

That was another painting she indulged me in creating that night: a starry sky, beneath which the resting earth, seemingly revitalising an inherent truth of eternity and our existence as well. But one thing that I must tell you here is that by those days, when I was frantically searching for her, wandering over the beaches, quite unexpectedly, I started to feel something different, that I was not alone. Rather, an invisible, powerful energy was always guiding my entity, making me feel I could flourish within and create what my soul yearns for.

I did not know why, but, quite surprisingly, during those moments, I gained a different insight that helped me prepare for a higher revelation. I got to know that I am not on this planet to be a banker, but I am destined for something else. I knew in my heart that the journey I was going through was not only a journey of excruciating pain, but a journey of gaining wisdom, aligning myself with my true spiritual centre that I once lost.

I made the decision to change my life once again, to respond to that higher calling and allow my inner artist to flow in a natural way. As a result of that, I wrote this piece with such feelings that I used to harbour deep in my heart:

Beneath the starry sky
As the earth rests for a while,
The mist casts off her spell —
A tiny creature only looks back,
Back to its insignificance;

Mourns for a while,
Then moves beyond –
Beyond this world of tangibility
Where only art may come with some
Special words; those words of eternity!

In this connection, I would like to remind you all that this was simply an incident that happened to that lady in particular. This does not mean that you all have that same poetic feeling inside that inspires you to be a poet, because it is barely possible for you all. But let me assure you one thing. Though you are not a poet, remember you all have that creator inside. Never allow that creator to be disheartened. Let us try to feel what she is trying to tell you intuitively, because your life itself may not sustain without that creator. She is the source of your imagination, your inspiration, the guiding principle of your being. She is someone like Aladdin's genie who always helps you to think beyond, to feel the world not in the way it is, but the way it may be, or sometimes the way it could be. She will never let you feel alone. Whenever you feel so, she will come and whisper into your ears. Let us pay heed to her gentle whispers. She is still humming around:

If the world seems to you a barren one, why do you not paint on it? Let's paint those colours that you once brought from that secret place of your heart, beyond this mundane world, once again to paint your shapeless form.

14| Deconstruct the Enigma You Possess Within

I know you're tired enough,
Stuck on something –
Wandering over the beach,
Just to have a gift;
Yet, finding no one, nothing
to give you that shift...

At first glance, this poem that I leave here unfinished may make you feel overwhelmed. What am I talking about? What is this enigma, and what are you searching for, wandering over the beach? It may also make you feel as though this is the enigma itself, to wander over the beach and beseech before everyone to get that special kind of gift that you've yearned for, for a long time. The question may remain unresolved until I break this enigmatic spell around you and help you to probe deep into the corner of yourself in a more explorative way, where you may find some layers of inconsistencies, but in spite of those multiple layers of uncertainties, you may also feel the essence of an ideal meaning that is universal and buried deep inside your entity since the primordial time of your existence. It may not appear in a tangible way, in a linear way or any structural pattern, but you can feel its very presence within your being as a source of inspiration that is always whispering into your ears not to be stuck where you are, but to inspire yourself in order to bring that much awaited metamorphosis within your being, to be aligned to your higher calling for which you are destined. In this chapter, I would like to share with you an untold truth about your Inner Mind and her mysterious, magical power to create a new you.

An Utter Failure of Linear Thinking to Probe Deep into Your Psyche

As your inner mind is an independent source of energy, any monotheistic structural pattern would not suffice to analyse it. If you do so, it may hinder its independence, resulting in a form of chaos. Sometimes, it may be an issue when you are suffering from an unexplained case of self-betrayal: you yearn for something and get something starkly different, resulting in an existential crisis and related hopelessness. During that period, you may also perceive an invisible gap; some sort of miscommunication in the course of your daily life and belongings. And I think, at this very moment, you need to explore that enigma that is very much surrounded by your being, as well as by the entire universe beyond the realm of any definable reality. And here, its indefinability makes it very much perceptible in the world of nonlinear ways of thinking.

As we already know, our world is full of complexities and, as a result, pluralistic thought patterns and the differentiation of meanings have completely pervaded society and our daily lives on a larger scale. So, understanding this enigma, buried deep inside yourself as the inner core of your mind where your soul resides, is not like comprehending a general catastrophe that comes just before the climax; instead, it is an independent plot that knows no boundaries regarding when to raise the curtain or when to fall, yet simultaneously goes along with you wherever you go, sometimes to enjoy, sometimes to explore your inner workings when you are acting on this stage of your life, yet at the same time helping you to weave that plot in a subtle way with the deeper shades of your existence. Sometimes, the perceptibility occurs when a trail of thoughts comes in your way in the form of an unexpected introspection, sometimes with the help of images and symbols, sometimes through your intuitive knowledge, like a sudden flash of lightning. But you need not baffle at that very moment or make yourself stumble as a lonely wanderer. Instead, I will assure you that amidst these multiple shades of thoughts and multiple colours of indefinability, you may find the essential meaning of your existence that is beyond any ideas of linearity, yet has that magical power to lead yourself towards a fertile land of inner creation where only the soul can paint, the soul can share and the soul can touch those unfathomable corners of your being through a process of creation and re-creation.

Let's Have a Deconstructive Vision of Your Inner Mind

If you probe deep into the inner layers of your mind, you may gain a clear idea of its basic potentials and how it can lead you into an unknown territory of deeper realisation or a higher knowing that can recreate you once again, in a newer way.

While the word INNER itself connotes its own potentials, similarly, if you deconstruct the word MIND, you will find the following potentials in this four-lettered word.

M – Connotes its Multiple, magical potentials.

I – Connotes its Inspiring energy that continually pushes you towards different Innovativeness.

N – Connotes its yearning for Newness (on a higher level of realisation)

D – Connotes its potential as a Dynamic server that creates Change (in a transformative sense)

In the process of deconstructing your inner mind (where your soul resides), you should have an idea of its spontaneous, intrinsic flow, which has always been within you as your innate potential since your primordial existence. So, while I am talking about its multiple, magical potentials, I can assure you that any logical or linear way of thinking cannot interpret this notion because its multiplicities not only introduce before you an unknown wonderland to hover around, but also make you feel aligned with that unseen territory. Your simplistic interpretations and traditional thoughts may disperse you at that moment. As you probe deeper, several meanings may come to your mind, conflicts may come and go, yet you cannot restrict yourself from moving forward. And herein lies its mystery; the mystery of its continuity, the mystery of its independence, its infinite magical power to push you towards the region of self-knowing more in an explorative way.

In the case of its innovative potential, it always acts as an inspiring persona, never letting you feel baffled amidst the dispersal of meanings that you are experiencing at the moments of your existential crisis. Rather, it will invite you towards the gateway of an imaginal world in a more creative way, where symbols, images and metaphors are the only expressive pictures to be painted on the tapestry of your soul, igniting within you a higher passion to light up your candles (the candles of your being) that you once left behind.

In the case of its other potential as Newness, I would tell you that it always has a tendency to form you in a newer way amidst those multiple potentials scattered in different forms. It gives you that chance to grow and mature within, with the help of your inner potentials, once again, through a continuous process of inner probing and self-realisation. It also acts as a dynamic server to bridge the lacuna that sometimes you may feel in the form of depression, anxiety or unexplained pain, resulting in instability and emotional turmoil (perhaps the cause of your detachment from the ultimate source of divine energy). If you probe more into this inner land, you may feel that it is also helping you to discover a newer version of yourself where it acts as a transformative energy, where you can feel the essence of a newer you, but not at the cost of losing your essentialities amidst these variables, amidst that continuous change, instead picking up those variables to create a newer you. And now, this transformed you can only yearn to be united with the ultimate divine energy and find a way to be reconciled to your true being once again.

When Consciousness Meets the Horizon of Inner Knowing, Conflicts Can Only Choose to Be Blurred

To deconstruct this enigma in an explorative way, I would like to share an incident involving an IT professional who was very successful by the usual, competitive, and socially comparable success measures. She did not have any lack, apparently. Rather, she had everything that makes one's life joyful and acceptable in a luxurious way. She had a fair job and a superfluous salary to inhabit. But she had always been experiencing a kind of gap, quite unexpectedly, in spite of her apparently glittering lifestyle.

After a few days, things changed, and eventually she started avoiding her usual office work. Whenever asked by someone, she used to answer, "I do not feel like, today..."

After some days, her problem started to increase more, making her unable to sleep at night. There was no other option for her but to consult a psychoanalyst. When asked by him, on their first meeting, "So, what are you seeking? As I see, you have everything to make your life prosper...", for some time she remained silent, as if finding no answer to link the line, but after some time she naively replied, "I am seeking something to fill the gap, the lack I have been experiencing..." She paused for a while, then continued, "I do not know exactly what I am seeking, or for what reason I am feeling this lack."

The psychoanalyst listened to her every word, and then asked her politely, "Do you love to listen to music?" She startled a bit, but gently replied, "Usually, I do not have that much time, but off and on, I love to hear it." "Then try to listen to it every night, just prior to your sleep, or whenever you feel free," he suggested. "Is it going to help me sleep?" she asked, astonished. "Maybe. If not, then it may help you to get that special something you are seeking for and come to me after fifteen days," he suggested.

After fifteen days, when she came to his chamber, a change on her face was very much visible.
"So, how are you feeling now?" the psychologist asked.
"Much better," she replied.
"So, how is your work going?"
"Not better than before."
"But why? What happened, my dear?"
"Still, I am unable to find that special something, and it is troubling me a lot, sometimes blocking me from doing my work that I liked to do a few months ago," she replied.
"So you just liked to do it, never loved it, right?" he asked.
"No, it is not like that ... but..." she fumbled, but did not find any answer.

"Now, just do one thing. Whenever you are listening to your favourite music, try to concentrate on the work that you like to do. I think you will feel better, and this feeling may help you to love your work and do things accordingly..." he suggested, wishing her all the best.

After some days, during their third meeting, she informed him about an unexpected experience that happened to her. "Last night, as I was listening to one of my favourite songs, I got completely lost in myself. I was not even sure how long I was listening to that. Literally, I did not feel that much urge to sit in front of my laptop and prepare myself for the next day's presentation. Instead, I was just feeling the song, as if my whole entity was trying to merge with that, and within a few minutes, I felt that I was about to get that special something, but with a blink of an eye, it withered away, and I found myself once again, hopeless, sitting lonely on my armchair!"

"Can you tell me how you were feeling then?" he asked her.

"It cannot be expressed in words, but it was something absolutely magical!" she replied with tears in her eyes.

"Do not be disheartened, my dear. I think you are very close to that special thing. When you are listening to that song, just try to feel and perceive what you like to do at that special moment."

And truly, that much-awaited miracle happened after some days, when she came to his chamber with a painting in her hand.

"This is for you," she said, bringing a gentle smile to her face while delivering it to him.

The psychoanalyst only nodded his head, smiling, as if expecting that, and said, "So, I think this is your special thing, isn't it?"

"Absolutely! That heavenly one!" she screamed with joy.

Do you want to know what she painted on that? It was a marvellous painting of the sky; the sky of her imagination. Beneath that, a garden where a butterfly was flying to and fro, feeling its entity, glancing at the star that was shining bright and trying to share a special message for that transformed creature, perhaps at the same time.

When Self-Reflection Brings a Higher Form of Revelation

If you probe deep into this matter, you may perceive that the process the psychoanalyst applied to her was not to distract her but to make her feel the inner essence of her being —the real yearning of her soul — where her consciousness expanded into a different realm to answer her soul's calling.

But it does not mean that this process would be applicable to you all. But do not get disheartened; rather, try to fathom deep into your psyche. She may show you that perfect divine time to harvest yourself in a creative way. For that lady, it was a form of self-reflection, where her love of listening to music served as an external stimulus, helping her reinterpret what her inner essence was trying to say to her in a secretive way, allowing her heart to open with receptive energy.

Before this inner knowing, she was completely unaware of its significant power and indulged in juggling between two identities. While the external core of herself tried to inspire her to become a more successful engineer, the other part of her identity sought something beyond the ordinary or linear levels of interpretation.

Though at first she could not interpret that gap through her own linear or traditional thought patterns, this resulted in an existential crisis that ultimately began to trouble her both externally and internally. At this very moment, the psychoanalyst perceived her in a more compassionate way and helped her open her heart and touch the eternal grace of her being, so that her soul could speak to her without any hindrance.

And there, quite automatically, that much-awaited revelation came to her as a spontaneous flow of nature, germinating within her a meta-inspiring state of consciousness. That consciousness actually helped her to leave behind all the old thought patterns through which she used to feel herself as a halfway messenger, waiting at the crossroad and suffering from a gap or some sort of detachment.

This higher level of consciousness not only helped her to bridge that gap but also made her feel her true essence, the purpose that was very much aligned with her higher self and connected to the ultimate source of divine energy, always guiding and inspiring her in order to build a newer form of creation and recreation. And it is only at this stage that her soul leads her to believe she is not a stuck energy but an energy of continuity and transformation for a higher purpose.

You need not be surprised by this incident, as here, her painting itself symbolises that self-reflection (the butterfly glancing at the star) and transformative magic (the butterfly itself) that she had already treasured within.

An Emergence of a Happy Soul

While I am suggesting you deconstruct your enigma within, you need not be baffled, as deconstruction is not meant to make you feel deprived of your inherent essence, but to discover a new self-awareness through continuous probing into the deepest regions of your psyche.

While going through that process, you may feel a bit bewildered, but do not be disheartened, my dear, as you are entering an unknown territory, maybe to discover a newfound land with your newfound identity.

That unknown territory towards which you are going is nothing but a significant change that has already occurred within yourself. You may not see it, but you may feel its very presence through that continuous urge to connect your being with that ultimate source of divine energy where truth resides. And there, you will find your true purpose.

So, when you are doing such deep explorations, you are not only using your mind but also your inner enigma, which, quite surprisingly, helps you feel your soul's presence in an intuitive way. At that very moment, you may also feel a higher level of realisation that knows no boundaries of logic or rational ways of thinking, but only knows when to evolve and how to evolve in a magical way.

Now it is up to you whether you prefer to feel that enigma (lurking within since your primordial existence) and explore it for a higher purpose, or prefer to be stuck as a caterpillar. But I would remind you further that it is only the caterpillar that has the potential to rediscover itself as a beautiful butterfly! Now it is your choice. But if you listen to your soul's voice, you can definitely hear her soft mumblings that I left unfinished at the opening section of this chapter.

But I'll be there for you!
Just probe inside—
Find out your inner Star
and peep into that Door
That once you left, ajar!

15| Imperfection: A Newer Way to Evolve Yourself

Have you ever imagined seizing the clouds or imprisoning the air in a particular enclosure, in a small arena of perfect entrapment? What do you think? Is it really possible? Or is it just an illusion to think over? As I see it, it has been an illusion to be absolutely perfect in this world of creative imperfection. You may be baffled and think, 'Why am I considering this world the world of creative imperfection?'

Here in this chapter, I would like to explore that mystery that continually harks you back and makes you feel that you need to be perfect at any cost. But have you ever thought, while the universe itself is imperfectly creative and harmonious with its own essence, why should we need to be perfect according to that monotheistic yardstick of perfection? As we are all nothing but some souls in human forms, we are very much aligned with the universal source of creativity and intelligence.

Hence, we all have that individual power within, our soul's power that always speaks of our identity, our presence. Though it may be imperfect according to the stereotypical world of logical understanding, it cannot be imperfect according to our soul's choice, according to the spontaneity of our heart, which always seeks that peace within, seeks a newness different from the world, and always speaks for the truth and beauty of our existence. But nowadays we are forgetting that fact and every time seeking that absolute perfection, quite unknowingly starting to hobnob around some false hopes of extra glitter, ultimately inviting utter failure at every facet of our lives. In the due course of getting perfection, most of the time we forget about our own potentials and indulge ourselves more and more in that path of getting extra attention for being perfect.

Sometimes we succeed, but sometimes we fail, and again and again allow our self-created deprived self to consume all that menacing darkness of failures and misappropriations. But we never delve into that darkness of unending possibilities. Rather, we always tend to channelize our consciousness towards that elusive concept of perfection, towards that monotheistic logical understanding of being perfect at every cost. And once again, we invite failure, invite that gap into our lives, even being in this imperfectly harmonious world of bliss and beauty.

Yes, here lies the difference. Here lies the magic of considering yourself as a perfect one, even with the art of your imperfection. Yes, here lies the magic of your soul who knows no boundaries of perfection and imperfection, who only knows how to feel herself, how to meander around those untouched places of mystery and grace; here lies her actual enigma, who chooses to evolve herself in a newer way, in a way where every time creation comes around spontaneously and whispers into your ears, "Hey, is there anything that needs to be perfect?" You may not find any answer all at once, but you can feel within that creation does not need to be perfect, but needs to be spontaneous, mingled with truth and beauty, all in its essence.

Being an Imperfect One Is Nothing but a Blessing to Identify Your Real Self Within

In this contemporaneous world, when all the time we are seeking that absolute perfection, do you not feel that in the due course of seeking perfection, somehow we are losing our individuality? Most of the time, we ignore ourselves and indulge our consciousness to achieve that extra perfection, instead of channelizing it into a fruitful exploration of our true selves.

Sometimes we also get frustrated enough to know ourselves, and sometimes even frightened enough to show our real selves to the world. Sometimes we feel that we are not enough to present ourselves before the world.

As a result of that, day by day, we lose our confidence, and we start to forget who we really are. And quite automatically, we start to deck ourselves with the extra coating of being perfect. But unfortunately, we lose our ideal essence, what we already have as our own potential, totally ignoring the consciousness of our inner space and depriving our soul once again. Knowing ourselves and accepting who we actually are is nothing but being with our own, being with the universal source of intelligence with which we have been aligned since the primordial time of existence. But most of the time, we forget that and tempt ourselves to be more and more perfect in the logical sense of perfection.

As a result, once again, we deprive ourselves of knowing and feeling our soul in a deeper way. As I feel, not being able to accept who you really are is nothing, but depriving your spiritual being and alienating yourself from the bliss of life, the bliss of truth, and your being.

So, knowing yourself and accepting who you are is nothing but accepting your depth within, accepting your imperfections and shortcomings in a harmonious way, and healing your soul in a newer way to evolve yourself with your own glory, more deeply. Herein lies the magical potential of our depth within, which most of the time we ignore in pursuit of that perfection according to the yardstick of a linear, logical pattern. But the more you delve within that depth, the more I can assure you that you may feel the depth of your unconscious, the eternal voice of your soul where you may not find that stereotypical yardstick of perfection, may not find what the external world considers as perfect, but may feel that inner peace, that symphony within to which your heart is also attuned. And the more you delve within, the more you start to grow, evolve in a new way, and open yourself to the truth of your unique potential. Once again, you may start to deepen and nurture your soul, enlivening yourself to the beauty of your unconditional being, to the truth of your spontaneous consciousness that will never induce you to be in your veiled appearance, rather always inspire you to be in your own feathers, to be with your own presence: unveiled, spontaneous and independent.

Imperfection Is Nothing But a Gateway to Feel Your Creativity in a Newer Way

The more you concentrate on what you do not have, the more you indulge in the incongruences of your existence itself. The more you start to ignore your authentic nature, the more you can feel that you are losing your inner experiences. And the quintessence of your being quite automatically starts to fade away. And here at this juncture, I would like to remind you that our soul is very much independent in nature. She is beyond the linear understanding of perfection of this stereotypical world. She only chooses what she likes to choose. And the moment you accept who you really are, quite automatically, you start to evolve in your own way, in a way where spontaneity comes along with creativity. And it is only possible through the help of your acceptance power. The moment you start to accept yourself, the moment you can feel an automatic transformation within you, where nonlinear understanding starts to flow spontaneously, and the secret passageways of your soul start to evolve in a newer way. And descending into the depths of your unconscious, gradually you start to feel that you are not an imperfect one, but a soul indeed with some higher potential. That is why it is very much aligned with your true being.

And herein lies the actual magic of becoming who you really are. I feel it is not only a recognition of your higher power, but a reconciliation with your true self, where you need not to be bothered about achieving perfection, but rather to be aware of what your soul truly wishes for. As therein lies the real dimension of your being, the depth of your consciousness that always prefers to flourish in a way of fruitful construction. And then imperfection may not appear as some shortcomings, but something as a blessing itself to rekindle your soul's candle in a newer way. Moreover, it comes as a pure form of self-reflection, a revelation itself that ultimately leads you towards the path of choosing your actual purpose in this world of existence. I still remember those words of that painter who could not cope with the world of monotheistic logical understanding, where perfections were only to be considered as something stereotypically 'successful'. Yes, he was not that successful. But he was content within, with his art, with his own; actually with his real self. And that real self is absolutely aligned with his creation, with his painting. Though he was not that successful enough according to the yardstick of perfection, he was perfect within his own. And it was only that passion, that creative instinct that ultimately helped him to see beyond that lens of perfection, beyond that so-called thought pattern and made him believe in the miracle of life itself, once again.

The moment I start to paint something, the moment I used to feel in touch with that, the canvas and the brushes did not appear as some mere objects to play with, but something by the help of which I can explore myself, indulging me to feel that my creation is nothing, but a replica of my own; colours start to flow with their natural ease and the painting starts to create itself in a spontaneous flow of nature, in a way where I need not think about the perfections or the imperfections, but can feel an aligned force within to create something new and to be with the harmonious string of eternity itself!

Let Us Feel Your Soul's Voice and Feel Your Being, Once Again

Imperfection does not mean that you have nothing to give this world or that you are not enough or complete within. Rather, it means evolving yourself to your true potential, with newer colours where your shortcomings are not something to think over, but with the help of those shortcomings, you can ultimately realise the depth you already have within.

And herein lies the magic of knowing yourself in a deeper way, knowing the more within, knowing the roots of your being, knowing the ground of your existence. The rational understanding of a stereotypical mindset cannot cope with these infinite potentials; it cannot sustain the unseen world of your infinite potentials. And as a result of that, you may feel depressed at times. But I can assure you, the more you delve within the deeper core of your unconscious, the more you can feel that your consciousness is leading you towards the depth of that deepest region of your psyche, enlivening your spiritual being in a newer way, transforming your ordinary consciousness towards a newer dimension and making you feel that you are complete and content within yourself. So you need not seek any external appreciation according to the yardstick of perfection.

You are perfect with yourself; you are perfect with all your imperfections as well. You are perfect to heal yourself and to heal others in a constructive way. Then your being will be perfectly attuned to that higher consciousness that will introduce before you your soul's ability. And at that state, your soul quite automatically starts to talk with your higher self, and gradually you start to feel that your imperfections are nothing, but another way to evolve, another way to present yourself before the world, simultaneously grounded, true to your being and deeply connected to the eternal truth of your existence.

And then only you can feel that even amidst the darkest of the dark, even in the midst of imperfections, you still have a hope, a creative force within to flourish in a newer way. And the more you delve into that dark, the more you can feel the power of your being; the truth of your existence, the purpose of your life itself. Once again, you start to feel that life is not all about seeking perfection; rather, it is about feeling your real self and being content and satisfied with reality.

And herein lies the celebration of your life stream, eternally flowing within since eternity, as this is the actual cognition, the real exploration of your soul's choice, and the reality that cannot be measured by that stereotypical yardstick of perfection. As our soul is always independent and spontaneous to create ordinary things in an extraordinary way, to transform imperfections into a newer way of perfection, where life may not seem as something of a failed masquerade, rather as something to flourish within with its celebratory grace!

If the darkest of the dark
Calls you back,
Makes you feel –
You've nothing to heal,
Delve into your heart, within
Bring back that light inside,
Brimming, within, gleaming bright
Yes! With that everlasting shine!

16| Gratitude: A Way to Enlighten Yourself

Whenever around the dusk mottled corridors of my world of expectations, the material part of my being harks me back and shrieks in desire, "Where do I get that golden horse that I once cherished?" Every time, my entity reminds me to pause for a while, allowing my stumbling feet to rest for that night, and the answers come quite surprisingly in her gentle presence:

There would be a serendipitous encounter when your heart would be vast enough to greet that energy. There, you may not find that horse you chased after, nor may you find any tangible thing to cling to. But there you may perceive an eternal peace and harmony that your heart once wished for; then only a smile may come to your face. You may forget how much you have or not. Only serenity can be felt with your thankful heart, in its silent pace.

Here, in this section, I would like to lay bare the secret of that serendipitous encounter that brings a smile on your face. You may not see it in a tangible way, but it may inspire you once again to look forward with a happy heart, allowing you to perceive a higher contentment within and making you feel where lies the secret of being grateful ever, even if you do not have what you have been desiring for a long period of time.

Gratitude Always Brings Forth a Higher Vision of Self-Cognition

Gratitude is something that allows your consciousness to enter a different self-explorative state, from where you may have a different cognition of your own worth. It not only acts as a state of your mind but also as a state of your being, always leading you towards a different territory of your roots and inspiring you to align with your true spiritual purpose. When expectations come along, your ego self can do nothing but falter your existence. Then gratitude may be your only saviour to inspire you to contemplate whatever you have. It once again may stir your energy to perceive that integrity your soul has been wishing for, maybe since the time of eternity when your being had been seeking some solace, some eternal harmony to adore. It may never indulge you to stand at a complaint counter and make a never-ending list of whatever you do not have, rather always inspire you to be thankful for what you have in this lifetime:

Along the dusty road,
Where you`ve nothing but
Only pebbles to confront
Never try to complain, but
Be thankful in your heart
That still you`ve that faith enough
To move beyond;
And to overcome those!
To enjoy that shift, that precious thing
That God is going to give you,
Maybe, as an eternal gift!

Always remember, a thankful heart is a hundred times better than an overambitious, regretful one. It has an eternal ability to see beyond the present circumstances, yet living in the present, feeling and enjoying the present moment as it comes. It does not have any regret for the past or those aspirations for a better future. Rather, it always makes you feel blessed, guiding you to discover a better version of yourself, to be more creative and productive. Endless expectations and their related frustrations may only lead you towards an unknown world of dissatisfactions from where you only find yourself as a helpless, complaining creature hopelessly wandering here and there in search of something better, but never finding that special something that would make you feel happy within. You may find a thousand reasons to be dissatisfied, but if you probe deep into your heart and adopt the grace of gratitude, you may feel a different, inspiring energy, always guiding you toward a peaceful, harmonious way.

And here lies the secret of being grateful, of being grounded with whatever you have, and of being thankful for whatever you have escaped in this lifetime, according to the divine order. As I feel, rejection is always a protection and, to some extent, a redirection towards a higher level for accomplishing something greater, something true to your soul's purpose.

But being grateful does not mean ceasing all your efforts and remaining completely idle, unaware of your ideal purpose on this planet. Rather, being grateful tells you a different story: to align with your true purpose, which your soul knows since the primordial time of your existence. It will never allow you to stop your journey; rather, it will always inspire you to move on for a special purpose, in accordance with the law of life and the law of continuity, keeping complete faith in God's grace. It never lets you feel overwhelmed by some unforeseen ambitions, but always deepens your belief system with a powerful divine magic that, in spite of numerous ups and downs, always helps you to behold a mirror before yourself, allowing you to contemplate more in a self-reflective way, where only your soul can have that ability to feel the truth of life itself.

It Allows Your Consciousness to Surrender to the Divine Intelligence

When gratitude comes, it not only helps you to grow emotionally, but also inspires you to enlighten your being from a spiritual dimension, from where life is not to be viewed as a mere search for some fruitless expectations, but a revelation with your soul that always guides you to tread in the right direction, on a special journey of harmony and acceptance. Here, acceptance does not mean to accept something under some pressure or compulsion, but here acceptance comes along with a deeper sense of faith and assurance, an assurance that can only come forward with a thankful heart. And there you may never place yourself to grieve over the past sorrows, but rather allow your soul to lift your heart for a better tomorrow in a harmonious and fruitful way.

Gratitude always leads you to enliven the depth of your being in a miraculous way. Remember, whenever you are feeling grateful from the core of your heart, it not only expands your vision but also always acts as a bridge for a higher level of communication, a communication between your higher self and the divine intelligence. It may be a bit awe-striking at the very first place, but if you probe deep into your heart, you may have a vision of perceiving a higher truth, the different truth of your life that always speaks of a complete surrender to the divine intelligence.

It also has a healing power to channelize your unconscious towards a different realm of realisation from where every thought of doubt and uncertainty quite automatically starts to fade away and you may once again start to feel that being thankful is nothing but allowing your soul to be rejuvenated and aligning her with her destined purpose, according to the divine grace. It has a miraculous power to open up the doors towards an unknown destination where something may be created out of nothing and nothing may also be viewed as something, not being lured with the thought of expectancy, but with the thought of some higher belief, a belief where only truth resides in a peaceful, harmonious way. In a way, it empowers your soul and enlightens your being to be in accord with the divine intelligence that surrounds your being and the entire universe as well:

The stars burn, melt themselves,
To bring the light, to make you feel
Serene and safe!
Patience comes forward
To assist them,
But they burn and burn themselves,
Smiling still-
For what we don`t know,
Is it something they want to heal?
Desire comes but moves backward,
Sneers a bit,
"How long would you melt yourselves?"
Their flames ask;
"How long my dear? Do you need some help?"
There is no one to answer,
Only silence comes.
Then all at once, their gratitude answers,
Breaking that silence;
"We`re still here to adopt
Our destined place!
To nurture ourselves,
With an eternal grace!"

When a Grateful Heart Knows All the Answers

A thankful heart is always a blessing in itself. Whenever you get stuck with unavoidable questions in this materialistic world, never feel gloomy; rather, try to say 'Thank you' just once, even in a whisper. And let us feel the magic! In this section, I am trying to sort out those questions that sometimes arise in our minds whenever we get stuck in the labyrinthine tunnels of hopeless desires and the related dissatisfactions:

If any question comes from your ambitious self, like, "Why am I failing again and again, in spite of all my diligence?" Let that answer come from your thankful self; "Maybe that was not the right direction for me. Redirection is always better, and I would rather consider it as a blessing for which I am destined on this planet."

If your impatient self asks, "How long should I have to wait as I am about to cross the finish line?" your thankful heart would console him and answer, "Still, I am thankful for the divine for preparing me for this journey. I have learned a lot. And now this waiting is a blessing in disguise!"

Sometimes your overwhelming self may stumble, may not find any other track to move further and desperately ask you, "How long should I have to continue? How long will it take to reach that destination?" Never feel disheartened, but rather try to listen to the gentle whispers coming from the depths of your heart. There you may find your thankful heart, mumbling softly, "I am already at my destination. I am content within. I have achieved a lot, and nothing external is required now to make me strong!"

If in this material world of continuous, superficial progression, the dissatisfied self comes to your doorstep and asks, "Nothing is permanent. So, what am I looking for? Why am I engaging myself to secure my future, as everything is impermanent in this mundane world?"

Your thankful heart may readily knock you once again and rekindle your spirit with her gentle note; "Acceptance has an eternal glory in itself when something is accepted in the light of an eternal truth. And here the truth is the truth of your life, your existence as well, that has a continuity within itself."

Sometimes your ego self may also come forward to ask you one simple question: "Where lies the reason for being grateful to other circumstances, while everything is achieved by my own strength?" Then your thankful self, once again, would ask you to pause for a while and calm your heart with a sweet note: *"It is because of the inner strength you have that you are able to do so. If you are not thankful enough, that means you are distancing yourself from God's grace (that is all-pervading and abundant). Hence, it is not because of you that you have achieved such success; it is because of the divine power surrounding your essence that you are still on the right track."*

Try To Be Thankful and Feel the Divinity within Your Being

In this section, I would like to share with you how the miraculous power of gratitude had entirely changed one's vision, healed her heart, and helped her believe in herself once again, in a different dimension of life, in a higher truth. And that truth is to surrender yourself completely to the divine intelligence in spite of losing everything. During my last visit to Pondicherry, as I stayed there for a couple of weeks, I fortunately encountered a lady who made me feel that gratitude is not something to philosophise but something to experience from the core of your heart, allowing your soul to feel your life as an eternal journey and believing in the divine power of the universe.

At every dawn, reaching the beach, she used to stand in front of the sea for a while, closing her eyes and mumbling something inaudible. After that, she used to open her eyes with a satisfactory smile on her face, perhaps to greet another morning with all its habitual charm and grace. Though, for the first few days, her actions were totally incomprehensible to me. But as the days passed by, my intuition began to feel that there must be something special in her actions, beyond the knowledge of our tangible understanding.

And trust me, I was not wrong in my perception. Those soft mumbles that she used to whisper at every dawn, standing on the beach, closing her eyes, were nothing but some thankful notes delivered to the universe. When asked by some of my friends, "What brings you here to thank the universe? Why do you do so?", while she had already lost everything, including her family and her last hope of finding any shelter, she neither felt startled at that moment nor embarrassed, but rather smiled and gently nodded her head. She took a deep breath and stared at the sky for a while, then continued:

But still I'm grateful to my creator. Maybe he has some other plans for me to share! I'm here only to thank that special energy that helped me learn to live despite losing everything. I'm here to thank that higher source of intelligence that inspires me to learn something beyond this tangible world of self-absorption. I'm here to thank that energy that made me believe once again how to live in this wonderful world without expecting anything from anyone, but to be thankful for whatever I have. I'm here only to thank that eternal divine energy that enlivened me to perceive my life as a blissful journey without any despair, without any dissatisfaction. I'm here to thank that special energy that helped me to behold the eternal truth of life.

She paused for a moment, staring at those waves coming and hitting the shore incessantly, perhaps reminiscing about something and then closed her eyes once again, maybe allowing her soul to feel the divinity, even while living in this mundane world. The vast expansion, perhaps, was listening to her soft whispers, allowing the clouds to float across the sky in a spontaneous way. The sun was gradually rising above, radiating its energy over the eastern sky once again to make her feel that her existence on this planet is nothing but a blessed one to perceive.

On that day, I realised that the vast expansion overhead is not only a shelter to nourish our wounded souls, but also always reminds us that there is still something special for us to be grateful for. And that special something is nothing but our own eternal existence on this planet. Being thankful is another way of embracing that existence, feeling that divinity once again within your mundane self.

That was our last day in Pondicherry. Years passed. Later, we were informed that her faith in divine order not only helped her rekindle hope but also prepared her to rebuild her foundation, allowing some miracles to happen in her world of reality.

In this connection, I would like to tell you that in this world of material prosperity, you may find numerous reasons to be grateful or regretful. But always try to remember one thing: the universe always prefers the grateful ones and listens to them patiently.

Are you still thinking of leading your life at the complaint counter as some regretful creatures? Or thinking of leading your life as an eternal journey of gratitude where a complete surrender to the divine is required. Now the choice is yours. I can only show you the way. But you have to tread on the right one, whatever you think, suits you.

17 | Prayer: A Secret Code of an Innocent but Powerful Soul

Does the title of this chapter seem to you like an antithesis? Or is it like an utterly impossible idea for you to mingle innocence and power at the same time? If you are fumbling a bit and have not been able to perceive the matter in a real sense, satisfying both your heart and soul, I would say, don't get bothered. Rather, try to feel the mystery of that innocence, the purity and truth that are already buried under the layer of your external conscious self.

If this appears before you as a self-contradiction and wavers your mind awhile, propelling you to think how you get that balance within, being innocent and powerful at the same time, I would rather assure you that herein lies the mystery itself, the mystery of your being, the truth of your existence and the beauty of your soul that is innocent and powerful at the same time. The only thing is that you've to feel it with all your inner grace.

Time changes, circumstances change. Even we change ourselves according to that revolving time shift and changing scenarios. But we never question ourselves. What is that inner power guiding us continually to make that shift? Is it really a change or a growth within that sense, or an ideal evolvement towards a different realm in order to get something higher, beyond the range of our tangible perception?

Most of you prefer to think that you yourselves are responsible for this change or growth, whatever you say. There is no other one or any other force working behind your back. Though to some extent it has been true, if you probe deeper within, you may discover something different. Some of you may even feel that, in reality, being innocent and praying for something would be the most idiotic thing to do in this tough world of material prosperity.

If you are lingering over the thought of how a simple prayer with an innocent heart can make a wonder in your life, I would rather say to you that it is very simple to pray even being innocent at heart, as innocence is nothing but the quintessence of a powerful soul that is eternally connected to the highest truth, to that divine intelligence that surrounds the universe as well as our being in a miraculous way. So, what do you think, what is prayer? Is it clinging around and begging for something before someone? Or something like a secret code, bringing contentment within your heart, once perceived by that lady for whom nothing had been left except her life?

In this chapter, I would like to explore the mystery of how an innocent heart can also be proven powerful enough only through the act of complete surrender to the divine.

When Innocence Acts as a Secret Code to Get Your Inner Power Back

"In those days, life seemed to me only as a caricature of my own fragile existence. I didn't have any shelter or food to sustain myself, nor even that much assurance that I was going to have a better life once again. I was only in front of the remnants of my own house and with the heaps of some broken pieces that I used to keep at my sweet home just a few days ago. I had nowhere to go, no one to complain, except brooding over the loss that had happened on that unfortunate night. I had also lost my job and my family altogether due to the nasty tricks of some conspirators. No one came to help me out, except those who only came to inflict more pain upon me, sometimes labelling me as an idiot,

sometimes even considering my identity as a fruitless existence of an emotional fool'.

But I didn't know why, deep in my heart, I still believed that someday a miracle would happen to help me out of this turmoil. I never lost my hope altogether. On those nights when I didn't have anything except the starry sky overhead, and truly speaking, there was something magical in it. I didn't even know how to pray at that time or what to pray for, as I had already lost everything. I had nothing to lose except that innocence of my heart that may seem to others as something idiotic, but to me it was something very precious. But surprisingly, some magic started to happen within me, and within a very few days, I somehow began to realise that my innocence was simply giving me that power all through those nights to sustain, to feel the truth and eternity of that nocturnal silence, and to perceive that purity within. Gradually, I started to feel that I was not the same one who had once been betrayed and deprived by some conspirators, but someone who knew how to live in this tough world in spite of being betrayed, in spite of being innocent at heart but powerful at the same time. On those nights, I used to do nothing but simply close my eyes. I didn't even know how to pray at that time or what to pray for, as I had already lost everything, but I could feel a special energy surrounding my entity, very much connected to that innocence of my heart, inspiring me to perceive some special truth, the truth of my existence, the truth of my consciousness that was gradually getting aligned, somehow I felt, with the universal intelligence.

And that consciousness was telling me the secret of an innocent heart; the innocence that can easily transform itself into a powerful phoenix only through the act of prayer. And truly, it worked for me in a miraculous way. But that does not mean that circumstances changed altogether for my benefit, but that I changed myself, not at the cost of betraying or losing my innocence, but by regaining my power back through the art of prayer that gave me nothing but contentment, a purity within my heart to release all my burdens and helped me to realise where lies my true worth."

You may be surprised, how is it possible for one to change herself even while living in the midst of that terrible situation?

But I must tell you that it has not been so easy for her to change herself altogether. She didn't even expect something from the divine, didn't beg for anything. But simply closed her eyes and allowed her innocence to surrender to that universal intelligence, not to get anything but to release that pain and conflict and to perceive that there is a higher force around the universe beyond this tangible world of material prosperity who is listening and talking to her constantly, providing her innocence at the same time a different insight, a higher wisdom that she didn`t have during that time of her betrayal.

And herein lies the secret code of an innocent heart, the true worth of her simple prayer that brings about a powerful change within her, not to make a shift in the external world, but to explore something higher within, to survive like a true warrior, being powerful and truthful from the core of her heart.

Prayer, an Act to Retreat and Rejuvenate Your Innocence Once Again

Prayer is not something that you have to do sitting in a meditative poise or detaching yourself from the external world altogether, but something very much close to your heart and a gateway in order to align your higher self to the truth of your being, to the truth of your existence where your soul can have that special power to integrate newer seeds for your growth and evolvement. This act of prayer is nothing but a retreat for some time from your external conscious self, and exploring that long-lost innocence that you once used to cherish both in your external and internal world.

Never think that it is just a reverie-like state of your mind or an elusive image, only to waver you for a while. It is that state of mind where your soul can find peace and harmony, as she knows no boundaries and only knows how to be peaceful, leaving behind the overwhelming, anxiety-ridden thoughts of your conscious, rational ideas and rediscovering a different world to gain different wisdom and insight.

You may think of it as an imaginary world where the conscious reasoning part of your existence is not working any longer. But if you probe deep into it, into this imaginary world of soulfulness, you may feel a solitude you can never feel with your conscious self. Here, retreat does not mean to leave behind all the essentialities of your conscious existence, but here retreat means to move beyond all those baggage just for a while, planting some newer seeds of beliefs with the help of your innocent heart, completely surrendering to the divine and allowing your consciousness to be aligned with the higher consciousness that not only surrounds your being, but also surrounds the entire universe as well, and continually helps you to emerge before the world as a true believer who knows wherein lies the true worth of your existence.

Prayer is not only something to rejuvenate your innocence, but also a way to find some momentary respite. Rather, here it comes as your soul's true companion, bringing forth your imaginary power to create a newer version of yourself—to create your being as a whole, exploring your true potential in a newer way. It also acts as a source of your inspiration in order to create a newer world where your soul can feel and your soul can talk, and only your soul can reach that highest form of ideals and paint a rich tapestry of your true emergence, bringing a powerful change within, even in the face of any external turmoil.

A Password for the Half-Way Messengers to Recognise Themselves and Their True Creator

Here, the word 'halfway messenger' may catch your attention at once. You may even feel: how can this act of prayer become a happy password for these half-way messengers? To comprehend the matter, first you have to know who these half-way messengers are, why, and what they are searching for as their happy password. In this connection, some excerpts from a poem that I had written a few years ago, I would like to share with you all;

"They`re waiting, waiting for that Hour
But nothing came, no one to help
To free them up, to make them feel, they`re not in a tower
They brood over their sorrows; I don`t know why?
What do they want to borrow?
Time came with a shrill voice!
Years passed, they wait and wait!
Circumstances changed, but they never questioned
They just closed their eyes, most of the time...
To bring that happy hour, to feel the grace
To have that special shower
They didn`t type the word `bliss', on that gadget they had
But a magic happened, within!
An exchange, they felt
And the word got typed under their shell to make them feel
They`re free now, rather in bliss
This time in a happy bower for a divine grace to greet!"

I think you have got my point, to whom I am referring as these half-way messengers. Actually, we are all in this category, especially those of us who are in search of our identity, in search of a mirror to behold our true reflection, in spite of getting overwhelmed by our day-to-day activities. And here comes the utility of prayer, praying with the core of your heart, with that innocence that is very much aligned to the innocence and purity of the universal intelligence, to bring you back to your source, to that eternal essence that is your origin, your truth.

In a way, this act of prayer can be viewed as a two-way communication between your soul and your creator. This can also be felt as a newer form of creation where the ground of your being finds solace, a shelter without any bereavement, without any anxiety or any disequilibrium that generally we feel in our waking life as the halfway messengers. This special hour of surrendering your entity to the divine may make you feel complete within. You may also get some special messages within yourself with the help of your intuition. Truths will become clearer, and your label as a halfway messenger, quite surprisingly, may start to fade away. Rather, quite naturally, you may start to feel your own purpose, your own worth on this planet and be able to lead your consciousness towards a different territory from where you may no longer feel yourself as a deprived one, as a half way messenger, stumbling here and there to find your identity, but can feel some newer hopes to flourish your inner seed, to ground your being in a meaningful way where truth resides.

I feel that here lies the mystery of your existence, the mystery of your power centre, eternally connected to the universal divine intelligence. During this happy hour, while you are praying to the divine, you may not feel anything tangible, but a different realisation may come across your mind, helping you to ground yourself to your eternal cord, to feel the eternal meaning of your existence where you can feel that your heart is open enough to receive something more to have a higher perception of anything. You can see the truth in every aspect of your life, and from then on, life may not appear before you as a fruitless survival, but as something special where imagination and reality are blended together in a harmonious way, in a way where, through this process of self-exploration, you can get a greater insight to perceive a powerful dimension of your being. In that sense, this act of prayer may also help you to have a proper self-reflection where you can communicate with yourself in a more spontaneous way, releasing and sharing your thoughts and inner experiences with your creator and asking for His help in order to emerge in a newer form, true to your being, in order to reconcile with your creator at your true home for which you are longing, since eternity.

When It Acts as a Bridge to Feel Your Being and the Eternity Within

The real power of prayer can only be felt when it acts as an invisible bridge between our conscious and subconscious realms.

Here lies the mystery of it, the mystery of your soul's power that, in spite of its innocence, never loses her balance, her ideal track, and never allows you to forget your ideal purpose. It is that special time when your heart is open enough to lead your consciousness to the highest ideals, leaving behind all your anger, stress, and other negative emotions that usually hinder our path and make us feel like half-way messengers.

In a way, this prayer can also be interpreted as a magical interplay between your inner and outer world. Here, during this process, your conscious mind can only have a blueprint of something that you want to accomplish in your waking life. You only have a desire or wish to make it happen. And herein lies the art of a true prayer: it introduces you to a different world of mature contemplation that may ultimately help you grow your ordinary consciousness to a higher level, from which you can visualise something beyond this tangible world —something very much real, where truth resides. And here, at this stage, you can perceive wherein lies the mystery of your soul and how this prayer is helping you move forward as a secret code to regain all the innocence and purity of your inner seed. And herein comes the harmonious union of your conscious and subconscious mind, leaving behind all the upheavals and preparing you to surrender to the divine to feel that eternity, that solace within.

Sometimes, this process of prayer may appear before you as a revelation, a revelation that can help you to see within, to realise a deeper dimension of reality both psychologically and spiritually. And this encounter with the divine cannot be possible in a state of mind when you yourself are totally bounded with your negative and egoistic thought patterns, rather it may be felt within your heart when you are entirely aligned to your higher self in order to feel that long lost innocence that already you have within, but in the daily course of conscious upheavals somehow lost it. Through this prayer, though you may not find anything tangible, you can feel a contentment within for perceiving a higher truth of reality, a truth where psychological barriers can be mended with the help of gaining different spiritual insights, not only to discover some greater, creative thoughts but also to feel an eternal bliss within.

I feel the gaining of this different spiritual insight may not be possible unless and until you can shed off your old ego self and see within in order to embrace that long lost innocence and purity that are already within you as your innate potentials, the true essence of your being. In that sense, this prayer not only helps you to find your original colours, but also makes you realise how to evolve like a powerful being instead of remaining innocent and pure at heart. And I feel herein lies the miracle of a true prayer, the power of an innocent heart and the purity and truth of a thankful soul.

It is a vast sea around/ I am swimming across the waves/ they are coming one after another/ I do not know which way/ they want me to sway/ I cannot close my eyes off/ as I am scared a lot/ the sky is turning grey, I feel/ but I do not know/ who is going me to heal/ I try to open up my eyes/ sometimes glancing at the sky/ sometimes I sigh/ The sky is wide enough, I feel/ how can I reach to His infinite/ still I am swimming across the sea/ still not getting that lighthouse/ I need to reach/ not even that bridge/ from where I can have His infinite/ I start to dive more into the deep/ but this time I have found something/ a precious gem to hold, I think/ the waves are still hitting at the shore, I see/ but this time I have found/ my long lost symphony.

This is a poem that I had written many years back, while I was also struggling to find my own identity. That time, I could not write the entire part of it. It took a few more months to find that precious gem I was searching for. And I think you can better understand which precious gem I am talking about. It was proved to me as a secret code to bring me back to my real existence, to make me realise the ground of my being. And that precious gem was nothing but my urge to explore myself with the help of this prayer, surrendering myself completely to the divine.

Now, Let's Pray with All Your Innocence and See the Magic Within

Do you want to know where lies the greatest power of being innocent at your heart and praying to the divine? In this section, I would like to lay bare that secret that may help you to know that deeper dimension of your being and how it is connected to the divine through the art of prayer.

Yes! This act of prayer is also a form of art itself. Here, through this art, you can create yourself once again in a new form, one very much aligned with your true self. At this very moment, you can feel yourself as a true sculptor, sowing within yourself some extraordinary seeds of hope and desire and aligning your entity completely with the divine. It not only helps you ground your being but also helps you emerge into the world with true awareness. An awareness that not only helps you to grow but also guides you what to perceive and how to perceive the ultimate truth of harmony and peace within.

In this connection, I would like to say that an innocent heart is always free from overthinking, overanalysis and doubtfulness. And herein lies the magic of it, the magic of feeling eternity, the magic of gaining a transcendent perception, the magic of being a true believer where your innocence can no longer be felt as your weakness, rather a power, a strength of your soul that knows no boundaries of conflicts and dilemmas but has that magical ability to touch the highest ideals, the truth, the integrity to emerge before the world not only as a powerful being, but also as the blessed one like that lady, I discussed before who did not know how to pray or what to pray for, as she had already lost everything. But she never gave up her spirit. And that is why her soul never let her feel alone. She never asked for anything but used to stare at the sky while only tears rolled down her cheeks.

She could not say anything. Maybe it was her own way of praying to the divine, asking for help in her own innocent and peaceful way. But the fact is, she was not deprived at all. Her every prayer was answered by that universal intelligence quite miraculously, even ten times better than her previous circumstances, in which she had been before that fatal disaster.

In this connection, I would like to mention that this art of prayer is not something to be practised in a meditative poise, but rather something very much natural and spontaneous. As prayer is not a specific process you have to maintain to get any divine help, rather it is a way to foster greater self-reflection, grounding yourself, and feeling your entity more meaningfully, where enlightenment and self-healing come naturally. Prayer is nothing but nurturing and rejuvenating your soul in a different way, where you retreat from the outside world for a while, grounding and feeling the essence of your own being to identify the secret wish of your higher self:

"Those days actually came to me as a source of some higher revelation, sometimes like a clear window pane through which I could have that vision, very helpful for growing within. I used to wait every night to see that starry sky as the thirsty earth does!

Then I did not know why I started to feel like that. But I was quite sure of one thing. During that hour, I had been very much with myself. All the memories of past hurts, worries, and tensions suddenly started to fade away. And I started to feel only the truth, the purpose of my being. I did not apply any method to pray, did not beg before Him, but simply allowed my heart to surrender to the divine and ask for His guidance. And the silence of that night came to me as my only guide to make me feel compelled to probe deeper within.

And herein lies the usefulness of a truthful prayer from a thankful heart that does not need any methodical process to make it happen, rather needs only innocence of your heart and purity of your soul, where truth resides and strength comes in a natural way.

And I learned this secret of prayer from that lady, the day I met her at Pondicherry for the last time. That day, I learned from her where the true art of prayer lies and how you can make it happen in your day-to-day life.

Here I`m giving you some of the tips on how to pray and how to feel that special moment, not only as a retreat but also as a blessing, within:

- Here, the first thing you need to keep in mind is that prayer is not a specific process to be performed strategically; rather, it is a spontaneous way of opening your heart, releasing your mind, and feeling the vibration that comes directly from your higher self. And when you feel that vibration, you may automatically connect to that universal divine intelligence to which you're already connected, since the primordial time of existence. Then this moment of prayer will appear before you as an hour when eternity holds for a moment within your heart.
- During this moment, you may not feel fatigued or stressed out, rather you may feel an urge to surrender your entity before that divine intelligence where, through the help of your contemplation, you will be able to foresee something higher than your usual perception, and in a way you may also feel that your conscious mind is responding to that and acknowledging all the wisdom and power that you`ve gained through your subconscious.
- Gradually, you yourself can recognise where the truth of that infinite wisdom is and how it is connected to your being in a natural, harmonious way. In a way, it also guides your destiny towards a different realm where you may feel a magical journey with your own being and find the power within to flourish your inner seed once again.
- During this process, you need not close your eyes in a typical way. Just take a deep breath and try to relax yourself from the outside world until you get centred and find the integrity within yourself. You may also open your eyes and deep in your heart harbour that wish that you want to be accomplished in a divine order. The

most important thing is to ground yourself as an independent being and try to feel the divinity you already have within. You don't need to get overwhelmed; gently allow your heart to imagine that your every wish is being fulfilled in its own time. You may also feel this wonderful thought just prior to sleep, in a drowsy state, or sometimes whenever you're able to free yourself from the outside world during a moment of solitude.

- One of the most important things that you need to have in your mind is that during this entire period, you should be devoid of any contradictions or dilemmas; rather, you have to be very much affirmative and consistent in your thought process. Remember, the purity and innocence of your soul cannot tolerate any such contradictions; rather, she is very much aligned with truth and harmony and always seeks to evolve, transcend, and grow to a higher dimension, true to your existence.
- Whenever you're not getting any solution to your problem, never let yourself weaken your heart by simply saying, "If that were to ever happen, I'll be the happiest one." Here, the word 'if' has that doubt in itself. In place of indulging yourself in such doubtful thoughts, relax your mind and allow your imagination to flow in a harmonious way without any restraint of negativity, without any conflict, but simply listen to the words of your higher self and allow your destiny to bring some miracles with the help of your faithful imagination. And this faithful imagination can only come from an innocent yet powerful soul who knows well the secret of surrender to that divine guidance which is essential to explore the right answers in the right order, for the sake of your life, your existence as well.

In a real sense, prayer is not only a moment when you can feel the ultimate truth—the bliss within—but also an awareness that you're with yourself, with your inner grace. It's a time when your consciousness can lead you to explore yourself and the divine grace you have within since the primordial time of your existence. If you're walking your path as a lonely wanderer and finding no one to hold your hand, never feel disheartened, but allow your inner light to show you that path, to give you that company that may make you feel you're complete within, complete with all your innocence, all your purity. And a true prayer is never a waste of time, rather something to be treasured to evolve your being in a harmonious way. Walking through the labyrinthine tunnel when you may feel a bit baffled, let's try to deepen your faith with all the innocence you've within. Only then will this special moment appear before you as a moment of magical bliss and serenity!

18| Forgive the Haters, Enlighten Yourself

Sometimes, reality makes us visit another dimension of life, where the thoughts of our usual experiences may be awe struck for a moment, pause for a while, and quite unexpectedly, impel us to feel more in a contemplative way, leading our consciousness to find an uncommon sense of reality, where we may be surprised to see how one`s mundane self and divine self can intertwine together to make a magical harmony.

Such was an incident that I encountered during my fifteen-day stay at Pondicherry. There, in my surroundings, I came to know about a lady named Jenipher, who was professionally a spiritual healer with her own centre, A Healer`s Cottage, during those days. I did not know why, but some inner force was continually telling me to visit her cottage for a while since I reached over there. You may think what had been so special about her work that made me feel that way. But do not get impatient, my dear, as therein lies the magic itself that I was letting you know just at the beginning of this chapter.

I still remember that day I went to meet her. When I met her for the first time, I was deeply moved by her unusual calmness, even in the face of someone's continuous resentment towards her. "You need not worry at all, I will always be by your side, Joseph…" she said, while comforting an old man, nearly of her age, who was continually trying to draw her attention, yet never allowing himself to treat her in a respectful way. But surprisingly enough, that was not bringing any discomfort or irritation to her face. In spite of that person's bitterness towards her, she was still calm and benevolent as ever before.

And the way she was addressing him was simply enough for me to comprehend that this was the same person, that same Joseph, with whom she was deeply in love about twenty years back. I was not only moved but also deeply astonished to see her behaviour towards that person who once left her out in the cold and never looked back to see how she had been all through those years.

How is it possible for one to forget all about those incidents and engage herself to look after that same person in the same way after twenty years? Somehow, I could not make myself prepare to comprehend the matter. Some questions were still lingering in my mind, while her intuition suddenly got that, and she exclaimed in a surprising manner, "It is only because of him that today I am here, and you are also here at this cottage, my dear!" she said, leaving me only to glance at her with my startled face. I did not find any expression, but somehow managed to utter, "Is this the same person? I mean ..." I fumbled and chose to be silent. But that silence was enough for her to continue the secret that she had buried deep inside her for a long time, but never found anyone to share.

"Yes, it is true that Joseph is the same person who did not show any mercy to leave me out in the cold and push me towards that never-ending darkness from where survival can only be considered as a myth. In spite of that, when I plunged deep into that darkness, quite in a paradoxical way, I realised that Joseph`s betrayal was nothing but a stimulus to bring me back to my real self.

Though, for that particular time, the entire world had collapsed for me, as he abandoned our relationship for someone else. But I did not know where I got that strength. I started to feel a mysterious force within that came in a surprising way and guided me not only to heal that wound, but inspired me to build this cottage for those wounded souls who want to be loved and healed."

She paused for a moment, took a deep breath, and then started again:

"... during those painful nights, a divine guidance I always felt within my heart, propelling me to move forward. When I used to sit out on the porch late at night, sometimes to forget Joseph, sometimes to forgive my past, I never felt that divine guidance was leaving me altogether; rather, I always felt it as an energy of assurance and protection." She sighed.

"But how did you come together again? Are you still in love with him?"

I asked her in utter astonishment! She smiled gently, and then expressed only a few words at that moment;

"Maybe destiny brought us back together, maybe for an unknown reason or maybe to feel that divine guidance deep in our heart, to heal someone and to be healed once again. You may be surprised, but I am still in love with him. But this time, this love is not of passion and expectations, but of compassion and humanity that has that inherent power within to forgive and heal that same person who once abandoned you, but now is at stake!"

Though it was a dusky afternoon, I could still feel that tears were rolling down her cheeks. But I was sure enough that those tears were not like those of usual remorse or sorrow, but of a contentment that one can have only through the power of forgiveness (that always speaks for a higher level of love and compassion). That afternoon, we could not talk much. We were sitting side by side as the evening silently crawled over the garden only to make us feel as two blurry figures, expressing nothing but perceiving that silence for a moment to lay bare an implicit truth, the inherent truth of our existence wherein lies the law of nature that never allows us to sabotage ourselves for the sake of taking revenge on others, rather inspires us to stay calm, forgive those persons and evolve in a way that nature always wants us to be.

Accept the Truth and Cast Off the Spell of Your Ego

I know it would be quite difficult for you to forgive someone who had pushed you towards that darkest corner of a labyrinthine tunnel from where life seems to be only a morbid creature, aimlessly trying to figure out the true meaning of survival. You may even feel yourself as an abandoned object, loitering on this earth without any purpose, without any worth as before. Right at this moment, you may want to shriek or even reach out to that person to give him or her the lesson he or she deserves. Sometimes, you may be successful in doing so, if it is considered to be a success in a true sense of comprehension. But sometimes you cannot, and instead hopelessly engage yourself in building an elusive castle of your ego, not only to take revenge on that person but also to satisfy your false, shadow self that continually tempts you to take revenge on that person, keeping you unaware of the adversities that may hurt you in a paradoxical way. Though it is utterly difficult for you to forget all those incidents with the wink of an eye, let me assure you, I am not telling you to forget them altogether, but to forgive them, not for the sake of those haters but for yourself as well.

Whenever these thoughts of revenge come into your mind, just try to ask yourself some simple questions: "Is it truly relevant to take that revenge?" "Is this the ideal truth that you are seeking?" "Wherein lies that truth?" "Is this the real purpose of your existence on this planet?"

Here, my intention is not to baffle you any longer. But just try to think once. During the course of this thinking, your shadow self may hinder you again, making you feel, once again, like only a tool in your ego's hand that does nothing but provoke you to think in countless ways to plot against someone. But for God's sake, never allow yourself to do that. And even if you are thinking of doing so, you are not only sabotaging yourself but depriving your being of aligning with your true self, your eternal centre, the centre of your inherent life force. And therein lies the truth itself, the truth of one's soul, the truth of eternity as well.

Let's Surrender to the Divine and Discover the Best Version of Yourself

Some of you may think that forgiveness is nothing but an attribute that only some virtuous persons can possess within themselves. Though to some extent it has been true, I would rather tell you that forgiveness is not merely some sort of virtue that we already have, but an inherent strength of our soul that always leads us to grow within, to evolve not only on a psychological basis but also on a spiritual level from where life is all about searching within, descending down into the depth and discovering a new version of yourself that you have never seen before.

Whenever you are forgiving someone, it acts as a stimulus for you to find that inner truth, the balance within yourself that you may have lost in a fit of anger or resentment or during the time when you decide to take revenge on others, completely forgetting your true purpose on this planet, that is not taking revenge or plotting against someone else but identifying what the universe is trying to tell you while you are encountering those unforgivable incidents. Is it trying to inspire you to grow within? Or inspiring you once again to be aligned with your true spiritual centre that you once left behind?

Though on a conscious level you may think that being judgmental is far easier than being compassionate, your thoughts may change if you probe deeper. Then you may realise that, to feel your being in its true essence, you need to open your heart, release all thoughts of past hurts, and allow your soul to evolve through self-reflection. At this juncture, a poem that is coming into my mind right now, I would like to share with you:

While the flames of revenge will burn,
Melting you inside,
Never allow them to burn
For long, but peep inside,
There you may feel,
The nest of a dove
To heal your wound,
Maybe for a higher glide!

I think it would be wise enough to feel the essence of your inner seed, which has always been helping you recognise your inner worth and gently caressing your wounds, reminding you once again that the flames you are burning for others are not only burning them but also trying to engulf your entity as a whole. And while you are doing that, quite unconsciously, you are also unable to recognise yourself. And here comes the identity crisis that automatically propels you to feel like a hopeless creature, helplessly trapped inside the spell of your self-created inferno, from where you may not find any escape except playing the game named Tit for Tat.

But while you are thinking about your past traumas, the betrayals that once broke you into fragmented pieces, you are blocking your soul from moving forward. You are hindering her path once again to get that ideal manifestation that she longed for since eternity. Though to some extent it may be impossible for you to forget all those past injuries altogether, but when your soul, your eternal mate, continually wishes to move forward, breaking all the lineage of those past traumas, you cannot indulge in brooding over them for long. In this connection, I would rather suggest that if it is not possible to forgive those who have wronged you, just surrender yourself to the ultimate divine energy that surrounds the universe and your entity, and allow your soul to recreate itself once again in a newer, empowering way. And there, with the help of that self-recognition, you yourself may realise how to forgive others in order to enlighten yourself, not only for the sake of detoxifying others but for your own detoxification as well.

Now, Let's Enlighten Ourselves for a Newer Dawn

In this section, I would like to lay bare that implicit truth that once Jenipher and I felt while conversing at her Healers' cottage, but we paused for a while for an unknown reason and found ourselves as only two living entities, expressing nothing but contemplating a higher truth inside, the truth of empathy, the truth of love, the truth in the power of forgiving someone and the truth of humanity as well. But one more thing I also realised that day. That is the truth of life, the truth of continuity that your soul always yearns to have since the primordial time of your existence. And that is why you can never ignore her higher calling. She is continually trying to rejuvenate your inner self, preparing you to blur all those past injuries in the light of divine guidance. To make it comprehensible in a simpler way, I would suggest that forgiving someone is not an overnight project to accomplish, rather preparing your higher self to expand your consciousness towards that dimension from where you can only throw off all your animalistic vengeance against someone and channelize that higher energy towards that way where Gods love and benevolence are always waiting to introduce before you a different region of divinity and selflessness. And when you`ll reach that state of your mind, automatically you may have a feeling to pray (for some higher needs) not only for the sake of yourself but also for the sake of that person who once mistreated you in an unpleasant way. And if possible, at that very moment, try to believe in yourself, your inner worth. Try to trust the supreme power of God, inherent within your being.

Here I would like to tell you one simple thing: forgiveness is not only a state of mind you have had since eternity; rather, it is a form of protection from the divine that heals your soul in a spontaneous way, always wishing to have that tranquillity and peace inside. Though we are not aware of it in a tangible way, this very nature of forgiving someone we already possess within us. But we never allow ourselves to open our hearts and see what the universe is trying to tell us in a secretive way! If you pay heed to that, you may feel the presence of that divine energy that Jenipher once felt during the time of her disaster.

Whenever you are going through such a crisis, for someone else's fault inflicted upon you, remember one thing, my dear. Just try to trust the inherent power of your higher self that is eternally connected to that ultimate divine energy pervading the entire universe and responsible for this wonderful creation. Though on a primary level, you may not believe in it. You may even think it is only a fantasy to be lulled by. But trust me, this is not like that, but something higher than our habitual observations. If you want to feel that energy and heal yourself on your own, here I am giving you some suggestions. You can try these if they suit you:

- If possible, first try to sit under the open sky from where the vast expansion is clearly visible. If not, try to practise it in a room of your comfort, but definitely in a state of recluse. And remember one more thing that during that time you need to be very much grounded with your own being, both consciously and unconsciously.
- Now centre yourself. Take a deep breath. Let's try to feel at ease both in your mind and in your body as well. Now, try to feel that whatever happened in the past happened for a reason. The reason may be incomprehensible at first. But it will be revealed in its due course.
- Now ask yourself one simple question: Was that the right way for that person to treat you? Obviously, your answer will be 'No'. But let me assure you that this utterance is not coming from your Inner self. Instead, it is actually coming from your conscious self, or sometimes from your ego self. But do not get bothered! It is quite natural for all of us to have this answer.

Particularly while you are going through such unbearable pain for someone else, you cannot forgive him or her at first.

- But now, just try to probe deep into your mind, into the deepest region from where your consciousness always guides you to have a different vision. Now ask yourself one question: Is this the same you who once cherished something great? Or is this real you who is now ruminating over the past hurts, past regrets for not getting that chance enough to treat that person in the same way? If you are getting your answers, then it is great! Then I think your higher self is already aligned to that divine energy. But if not, then try to ask that divine energy. Ask for some help.
- Now let's pray for His assistance. Try to calm your mind and listen to your intuition. He will never guide you in the wrong way. First pray for yourself, then pray for those who once hurt you, pushed you towards those dark dungeons, pray for those who once disrespected you, pray for those who never treated you the way you deserve, pray for those whose hatred sometimes led you to take some unpleasant decisions, pray for those who judged you in a wrong way, pray even for those situations that once compelled you to do some fatal mistakes in your life.
- Now pause for a while. Take a deep breath and complete your prayer not with the hope that God is going to take care of all of your burdens and sorrows (though surely, He does that, as through this process of self-healing). Instead, complete it with a deep belief in the eternal healing power of the universe, with the belief that forgiving someone is not weakening your soul`s power but empowering it more with His divine grace and profound love. And in the process of doing so, you may feel that the vast expansion is listening to you and

preparing you once again for an enlightenment to feel the divinity within your being, once again, that your soul has always cherished since eternity.

- Now let's try to feel that you are forgiving them, not in an imaginative way, not in the way where fantasy comes along with the thoughts of our realities. And in the way where reality itself speaks of forgiveness, inviting a different world of humanity.

And herein lies, I think, the victory itself, the victory of your being that always prefers to be aligned with your true self, your true purpose. Though we all know what victory is or what it should be like, we never wished to comprehend it in a real sense. On a mere level of understanding, it may appear as a synonym of success, a word that we often like to utter in order to show our material accomplishments. But the actual essence of it lies elsewhere.

It does not mean in the way of taking revenge against someone for their deeds, not in the way of mourning over some past grief, but in the way while you are getting enlightened for a higher purpose of your life, leaving all the past traumas behind and moving on once again to embrace the highest truth that only the nature knows, like the truth of Healers Cottage` that was once built by that betrayed yet enlightened soul of Jenipher.

19| Let's Allow Your Feminine Self to Restore the Inner Balance

Sometimes, he comes to fly me up.
I get thrilled, yet overwhelmed a bit.
Which way does he want to lead me up?
Sometimes, I get puzzled myself,
Do not even know how to mend that puzzling self.
He wants to fly me up and up in the air,
But does not know which story exactly he wants to share.
But like a sudden revelation, she comes,
As the night creeps over the valley to heal it once again
With all her essence, with all her magical touch!

Only a cursory glance at this poem may make you feel wondered, but if you probe into it, you will get a different, yet deeper meaning that you are always facing in your day-to-day life. You may think, what is this feminine self I am talking about? Is this some special attribute that only women possess or something that we all have within, irrespective of our gender?

In this connection, I would like to tell you that this feminine self is nothing but the guiding principle of our life itself that we always tend to overlook in the course of our usual way of thinking. Some of you may feel that your life purpose is only to pursue some achievements that you cannot handle without being logical. Though, to some extent it has been true because rationality always gives you that support that you need to have in order to sustain in this material world.

But whenever you are confronted with any irreparable loss or with some dilemma in your life that is beyond any logical interpretations, you may pause for a while and get perturbed a bit. And only then, you can feel some mysterious yet gentle touch of a caressing energy, coming forward, quite surprisingly, from the depth of your heart to lift you up for a higher purpose that still remains unknown to you. And then, for the first time, you will get introduced to your feminine self. Then you may feel, what would be the ideal purpose of your life? Is it only in the pursuit of never-ending success? Or is it in the recognition of yourself that your feminine side is trying to show you in an intuitive way?

You may get puzzled again, and that energy seems to fade away with the wink of an eye! You may stand still, dumbfounded a bit, but you do not know how to evolve yourself. You may seek help from your logical conscious mind. But at that very moment, you may realise that your rational mind is also getting puzzled like yourself! Here, in this chapter, I would like to lay bare that implicit truth that your puzzling self is always searching for, but never finding in a rational way of understanding.

Repression of Your Feminine Self Always Leads You to a State of Existential Despair

In this section, I would like to tell you that I am not here to talk about gender disparity; we are all living bodies with our souls inside, since the primordial time of our existence, which serves as a secret energy to inspire us, irrespective of our gender. She always serves as a complementary part of our rational self in an intuitive manner. Whenever your masculine self gets tired, finding no proper track with his logical potential to find your inner worth, she always comes forward not only in a psychological way where your emotions can find their true colours to express, but in a spiritual way where you yourself can recognise your true being, your true purpose on this planet. So, whenever you are neglecting her soft whispers, you are not only repressing your heart's desire but repressing that higher consciousness within, which can lead you to meet the independent and interstitial flow of your soul, deep inside.

And in the course of this repression, you are not only blocking the paths of your psychological growth but also hindering all the potentials of your feminine self to flourish within, to create something new as per your soul's imagination. As a result of that, you yourself are inviting that stage of identity crisis in your life, in spite of being at the peak of your material success. You may frustrate yourself, mourn for a while, and ask yourself, "Is this the perfect way of living? So, what is causing me this emptiness?"

This same case held true for a businessman who never paid any heed to his heart's desires, never allowed himself to enjoy life with his friends and family, but always kept himself busy making money and pursuing for the overall success of his company. He never paid any attention to the needs and desires of his employees. He only ordered and asked them for production according to his demand. Within a few years, as a result of his stern behaviour, things started to get worse, and he faced an utter disaster when his employees started to revolt against him and threatened him that they would no longer be able to work for him amidst that inhuman work environment where human beings are categorised only in the form of some nine to five job attendants. That agitation of his employees literally shook the whole empire of his business. And as a result of that, his whole existence started to crumble down. He started to realise that a continuous repression of his heart's desires ultimately had turned him into a human machine. Because when he constructed that company, he not only invested in it his intellect and diligence but also poured his emotions as well. But afterwards, he forgot that feminine energy that worked for him behind the scenes during that time. And in the course of that realisation, he also felt that he had made a bigger mistake by betraying that energy that once supported him as a caring mother, only in order to gain material success, and that disastrous situation is nothing but the consequence of that self-betrayal. I still remember the final message that I listened from one of his employees to whom he shared his grief when he was in his own chamber, alone and finding his own faults in a depressive way:

"Truly, a balance was needed, within!"

Recognising Your Feminine Self Helps You to Connect to Your Spiritual Centre

Whenever our souls cry, she cries in an inaudible way, in a way where we are no longer aware that we are alive, but move our bodies from here to there, remaining unaware of the fact that we are only surviving, but not living with that spark of life. And it happens when you neglect your soul and indulge yourself in the pursuit of gaining material success. Though it does not happen for everyone, I think some of you may experience that inner cry of your soul when your tender heart tries to tell you something and you are doing something else.

If you think that this overindulgence in this feminine side may make you feel feeble and the outside world may consider you as a person of less intellect and power, I would assure you that this is not the right way to perceive this matter. Rather, you need to fathom deep into your heart. Let's pay some heed to that silent self. Is she trying to demotivate you? You may find the answers. But I would suggest, if you are finding those answers, try to find those not in a conscious way of reasoning but more in a transcendental way of perceiving your soul inside. Deep into your heart, you may feel her gentle yet majestic presence. You may also feel that she is not telling you to leave your intellect altogether, rather inspiring you to descend deep into the depths of your being and recognise your true power, inherent within you, very much essential to create and evolve yourself once again for a higher purpose, for a greater reason. Though gentle and caring in nature as the dove inside her nest, with a wink of an eye, she can transform herself into the phoenix to raise you up from the ashes. And herein lies the purpose of recognising your true spiritual centre from which you got separated in the course of enjoying or pursuing the glittering extravaganzas of your life in order to gain material success.

In this connection, I would like to suggest that this spiritual centre is nothing but the centre of your being, where your soul is truly aligned with a powerful divine energy that not only surrounds your being but also the entire universe. But whenever you are neglecting your feminine self, you are not only depriving yourself of that spiritual centre but also blocking the path of that divine energy to flow within yourself. And the immediate result to confront is only the dilemma in perceiving the matter of what you truly want and what you need to have to flourish in this beautiful world of creation.

Creation is not something that needs a definition in a logical way of understanding, but something that directly comes from your soul, allowing you to contemplate in a deeper way. And when this happens, you can feel an eternal bliss and tranquillity within yourself that allows your heart to breathe, to be aligned with that divine energy that may always inspire you to see the beauty of a silent night, where the darkness of the night bears a special message for a newer dawn.

A True Emergence of Yourself Always Needs a Proper Balance, Within

In this section, I would like to draw your attention to an incident that may reveal an implicit truth about the mysterious power of your feminine self and how she works within your being to enliven you. Because soul searching is a special journey in which one's outer layer of mind confronts the innermost depths of one's being.

And sometimes it channelizes one's consciousness towards a different realm where the only truth is to be aligned with the innermost core of your being, where there will be no gap in between the two layers of your mind, rather you can find yourself as a blissful entity, aligned with your true purpose that continually inspires you to move forward, not at the cost of sacrificing your masculine self but by bringing that balance within you, where your masculine self will no longer be able to hinder the path of your feminine self. Rather, with her help, he'll get to know at which point you need to transform yourself to flourish your entity once again with a newer approach, where your feminine self would not feel betrayed but find her own restoration in a creative way. And therein lies the meaning of your true existence.

In order to explicate it in a simpler way, here I am going to share with you an incident that happened with a lady named Sophia, five years back. I got to know about her from one of my psychologist friends who had treated her for about a year. A continuous repression of her feminine self quite unexpectedly had led her towards an utter state of depression that quite surprisingly kept her unaware of the fact that she was actually going through such a crisis. But the thought of repressing her emotions came to her when continuous humiliation from external society led her to feel she should be bolder and more courageous than men. Maybe somehow, this feeling of ameliorating herself to that so called social status led her to develop, within, quite unconsciously, a hard, masculine layer that continually prompted her to be more aggressive and strict than her original nature. She always tried to pretend that she was strong and confident enough. Though apparently, she had attained every success that a person can hardly have in his or her life, deep inside, she was suffering from a sorrow that led her towards that unpredictable state of depression. Now I am going to tell you her confession that she shared with my friend during the moment when she completely lost her feminine self on a mental state, but quite surprisingly was able to restore that once again with the help of my friend:

"During those long, tiring days, sometimes I used to show the world that I`m elated enough. But you need not think that I was happy within; rather, I start to feel happy from now on, as I believe that no one can harass or humiliate me like before.

I had everything to sustain me; I had everything that some of you might not even imagine in your whole life. I used to get myself busy at work, always trying to convince myself that I'm happy. But some unnatural feelings started to keep me awake at night. For the first few days, I felt it might be because of the unbearable work pressure I was going through during those days. But after a few days, things started to get worse. I immediately came to you for some consultations. You suggested, I think, that I contemplate more whenever I find any sort of recluse after a day's break. I used to do that, but I did not find what exactly was hindering my path. But somehow, I had an intuition that I was betraying myself; I was getting separated from a nourishing and caring energy that I once used to feel within.

Then something happened, just like a miracle. That was a calm night, the stars were glittering in the sky with their true spirits. I stood still under the sky and somehow started to feel a dimmed yet very graceful radiance gradually trying to descend to the earth, maybe trying to pour its grace on me too. And quite naturally, all those rigorous thoughts of achieving something greater than those who once bullied me started to fade away. I felt, deep in my heart, that someone, as a mother figure, was watching over me that night. She was like an eternal source of energy, calming me down, yet at the same time inspiring me to nurture that innocence, the purity of my heart that I once buried within, considering it as only a feeble form of my personality. And then I realised that she was not only inspiring me, but asking me to talk with my only friend, my only saviour, my feminine self, not to sustain in this world but to live in a graceful way where my soul will have that much space to flourish with spontaneity, without any hindrance.

You may be eager to know, did she quit her job after that realisation? But I would say, if you think so, you are absolutely interpreting it incorrectly. That recognition of her feminine self was needed for her to regain her balance and reconnect with the ideal essence she had left behind. And with the help of that self-reflection only, she was able to maintain her job in a peaceful way where she never needed to sacrifice her soul`s desires at the cost of gaining material success, rather it led her towards that direction where her feminine self ultimately succeeded in maintaining the balance with her logical masculine energy, enabling her to find a deeper understanding to recognise an eternal energy of her soul that knows no boundaries, knows no language of repression, but knows only the meaning of a higher cognition, of a higher creation.

20 | Sleep: A Divine Blessing to Heal Yourself

In this modern cybernetic age of progression and success, unfortunately, we're forgetting about an inevitable demand of our lives. And that demand is nothing but the need to take a break, to rest our heads and relax our nerves, to revitalise ourselves in a new way. And that rest is utterly impossible unless and until we go through a deep sleep and energise ourselves once again for the eternal flow of our life. But nowadays we are forgetting that need and consequently depriving ourselves of this eternal grace of God. And as a result of this sleep deprivation, we are not only facing severe insomnia problems, but sometimes it's also causing different psychotic disorders. As this deprivation is not a simple deprivation of sleep, but it's actually a deprivation, I feel, from God's eternal love and blessings.

And the moment you get separated from these eternal blessings, the moment you start to feel that there is some lack within your entity. And most of the time, you find yourself an irritable, less satisfied person, always searching for something better, but unfortunately never able to feel that contentment within! As deprivation of sleep is nothing but depriving yourself of that divine law, by the help of which your subconscious provides you with all the answers latent under the layer of your psyche. And herein lies the miraculous effect of sleep; the miraculous power of these infinite blessings that helps us to believe in our strength, helps to bring us back to our confidence and quite miraculously allows us to surrender to that supreme power of universal intelligence that is already within us. It also allows our subconscious to choose the right things in a divinely guided order.

What Is Sleep and Why Does It Come to Every Being

In simpler terms, sleep is that special moment when, during that time, you completely forget about everything. But in a deeper way to interpret, it can be considered that it's been that blessed rejuvenation, a wondrous process of withdrawing yourself from all of your conscious events for a certain period of time. For that duration, you're asleep, but your subconscious is very much alive within you.

Then the conscious mind is entirely in deep sleep, but your subconscious knows all the answers with its eternal magical power. And herein lies the wondrous power of these divine blessings. Yes! Herein lies its miracle, by the help of which the creative intelligence of your subconscious comes to the fore and once again, quite spontaneously, you get recharged with all your vitality, with all your power, hidden under the deeper core of your being.

This sleep is not only a process of withdrawing yourself from your conscious world for a while and forgetting about all the confusions and mishaps of your daily life for a certain period of time, but it is that divine blessings to rejuvenate yourself in a newer way, aligning your entity to be in full accord with your life force, inspiring you to believe that life is not about running all the time, but to rest, pause for a while and heal yourself to be in complete harmony. And that's why we are all blessed with this divine blessing since the time we came into our mortal existence on this earth. This is not a process only to rest your body and mind, but it is a necessity for every being to rest and rejuvenate their energy, and once again to prepare themselves to fit into this inevitable flow of life. Our subconscious never gets tired; it's always active. And that's why sleep is not a process to rest our body, but it's all about a spiritual regeneration through which we all are undergoing every night. And it is in this divinely orchestrated process that our soul is connected to that universal law of intelligence in order to welcome a peaceful vitality in our lives.

The Miraculous Power of Sleep

In a deeper sense, sleep has an enormous effect on rekindling your energy and making you feel blessed enough to be at peace with yourself and with the world, as well as your subconscious, which has that hidden power within and knows everything. And this sleep is that divine opportunity to talk with your subconscious that always prefers to guide you in a fruitful and constructive way. It is only through proper sleep that you will get to know where lies the infinite possibility of this subconscious that always guides you to move forward towards the truth of universal intelligence.

In order to interpret it in a deeper way, it may be said that sleep is nothing but a divinely guided medium to bring the infinite possibilities of your subconscious to the fore as our subconscious is very wise. It knows everything about what is going to happen in our future realm. And sometimes, through sleep, it tells us of our future. Sometimes it also protects and guides us from all kinds of mishaps.

As it happened to that wildlife photographer with whom one of my friends met during his stay in Nepal. Actually, during one of his shoots at Masai Mara, he had completely lost his way altogether. The road map that he had with him during that trip was completely unable to show him the right path to proceed. To put it in his words, it would be like:

"It was really like a labyrinthine maze for me. I did not have that much food or water. The scorching heat was just blazing out with all its enormous tenacity. My skin was getting burnt; my lips were searching for some water, at least to quench my thirst. I was feeling

helpless. But I did not know how I fell asleep in that dark tunnel I was crossing through. But when I awoke on that morning, everything seemed to me as clear as the light of a blessed day, and right at that very moment, I realised what had been the exact direction to reach my destination. Yes! It was all through that deep sleep I got to know the exact location where I needed to reach on that particular day. I thanked my subconscious, thanked the Almighty."

Yes! Herein lies the miracle of this divine blessing: the creative manifesting power of our subconscious that knows everything. Herein lies the latent power of our inner self that sleep can bring along with its caressing touch, with its touch of shelter and protection.

Sleep Has a Healing Effect to Heal Your Heart and Soothe Your Mind

Proper sleep is nothing but a divine blessing in itself to rejuvenate your heart and make you believe in the miraculous power of your subconscious once again. It not only comes to every being on this planet in order to soothe your mind, but it also comes to heal your soul once again, allowing you to cherish the flow of life in a spontaneous way.

In a way, it comes as a counsel to soothe your mind and allow your subconscious to choose the right things in the right order. And moreover, it helps you to be grounded in your being, in your centre once again, and to believe in the infinite and miraculous power of your subconscious as an eternal process towards life.

"It was all for that divine blessing. It was all for that sleep, once again I started to feel that I am here to live my life, not to couch myself under a tattered shell, but to breathe, heal myself and to ensure my soul that I am here with her not to be humiliated, but to dance with her in joy, dangling my wings and accepting all the newer colours of life, quite like a butterfly after its magical transformation."

It was a confession of a young girl who had undergone through a severe traumatic experience in her love life that even led her to end her life.

"It actually broke me into pieces. I was in search of where I should find those broken pieces to mend up. I used to sleep for long, long hours. For the very first few days nothing happened to soothe my heart; rather, it was all that sinister darkness trying to engulf my entity altogether.

But after some days I realised that this sleep was actually helping me to forget all those mishaps. It was not only healing me but also allowing my entity to flourish in a newer way. And still now I remember, the more I used to sleep in those days, the more I used to get aligned with my true purpose, I felt. Actually in those hours I did nothing but used to close my eyes, sleep to lull my entity and surrender myself completely to the divine. Just prior to sleep, I used to say to myself that I am not alone, but the divine is watching over me and protecting me with all His purity and bliss. And trust me, within a few days I started to feel that all those bad memories quite automatically were fading away, much like those vapours left to be considered as some oblivion!"

She paused for a while, closing her eyes, and reminiscing about something. Then continued:

"It was all because of that deep sleep; my soul had been able to help me out once again, had been able to heal me from that disaster, and to conjure up the right things in a divinely blessed manner!" And yes! Herein lies the magic of sleeping in a peaceful way. Herein lies the efficacy of surrendering your entity completely towards that universal source of divine intelligence in a soulful and blissful manner. Here, the sleep comes as a form of prayer itself, somewhat more like a divine law. And in that blessed moment, your conscious mind completely withdraws itself from the vexations of this sensory world, and your subconscious helps you to be with the creative intelligence you have within, since the primordial time of your existence.

And this regular withdrawal from all the conscious forms of confusion actually helps you not only to rest your heart and mind, but also to heal yourself once again to be aligned with your true purpose. A proper sleep is nothing but a spiritual regeneration itself that not only brings good counsel, but also rejuvenates your infinite intelligence in order to recognise your hidden abilities in a divinely blessed manner. Yes! Sleep is nothing but a blessing from the universal source of divine intelligence to manifest all your wishes, allowing your soul to make those happen in a blissful accord.

In a deeper way to interpret it, it is that divine law, sent from the universe to all levels of being, not only to rest our weary body to refresh itself, but also to rejuvenate our inner being to the truth of divine intelligence. In a way, it is to be considered as some precious pearl in the midst of our reckless lives. It is that serenity that comes every night to behold our inner beauty once again and to make us feel that we are here on this beautiful planet, to feel the peace within, to heal our souls, and to nurture our being in a divine accord.

Yes! This sleep can only provide that divine peace, even being in this mortal body of survival and continuous struggle. And it is only with the help of this sleep that the inner experience of your psyche feels a balance within, and quite automatically, you get aligned with that deeper truth of your existence. And that is why healing comes in its natural course, and your soul ultimately gets that relief to flourish in its own way of independence and spontaneity.

In a way, sleep comes as a blessing to those wounded souls who have suffered greatly but finally plead for emancipation; it is nothing but a healing to those betrayed souls who did not find any diagnostic measure to heal themselves but now plead before God for help. I still remember that young lady's words whom I met that day for the last time; *"I did not know how sleep used to come to me in those days. Still, I cannot remember that any more. But later I realised that it was all a divine help that I had been asking for… quite automatically my dwindling eyes used to get relaxed. A deep peace and serenity started to cover up my entity and a great calmness started to prevail within me in its blissful serenity. Yes! It was only that divine blessing, sleep itself, that brought that solace and serenity to heal me from all kinds of oddities and mishaps. I used to close my eyes, take a deep breath, and mumble some simple words: 'God, please help!' It was nothing but more like a surrender to me; a surrender to that divine shelter, a surrender to that infinite abundance from where I came and will be merged into!*

Sleep in Peace and Wake Up to Feel the Wonder of Life, Once Again

In this modern age of cybernetic progress, insomnia has already wrapped its tentacles around the world. Nowadays, it has become our habit to avoid sleep altogether and engage ourselves more in our late-night work. But at this juncture, I would like to remind you all that sleep is not something to be relaxed for, but a divine blessing itself to heal and soothe your body and mind, make you believe in your infinite possibilities, and allow your subconscious to be the best guide for yourself.

It is not only essential to bring that peace and joy into your waking life, but also to strengthen your memory and to allow your subconscious to work in a properly constructive way. Sleep deprivation not only causes depression and anxiety, but also leads towards a state of psychotic breakdown, from where even the true purpose of one's life may start to appear meaningless. Actually, sleep brings counsel to those wounded souls who need this surrender. Sleep comes to them as an opportunity to surrender themselves to that divine intelligence, allowing their subconscious to work in the right order in a divinely blessed, blissful accord.

If the journey of our life is a spiritual one to explore ourselves, sleep is nothing but a special touch in this beautiful journey to manifest our energy in a new way. As the tendency of our subconscious is always towards that divine intelligence, here sleep comes as a silent protector to rejuvenate your being, allowing your soul to return to the truth of that higher purpose once again, strengthening your entity in a new way to behold your beauty and your grace not only within yourself, but also to present that grace before the world in a magical way.

And herein lies the wonder of our being; the wonder of our universal intelligence as well. Herein lies the wonder of our subconscious, which never stops for a moment but all the time guides and protects us as a divine protector. In a deeper way to interpret it, it is to be said that sleep is that powerful opportunity sent from the divine intelligence not only to strengthen your being, true to your existence, but to allow your soul to flourish in her own way.

Yes, in a deeper way to contemplate, sleep is nothing but a gateway—a medium to connect to that universal source of intelligence, even once a day. And not even a single being is deprived of this beautiful blessing. Herein lies the wonder of our existence, the miracle of the creation of God as well. Herein lies the power of your sustenance, the joy of your life and that eternal grace and beauty you seek everywhere, every time.

So, your time starts now. What would you like to choose? A tiring, sleepless day with lots of so-called success and nuisances, or a day with proper sleep, full of joy and happiness with greater achievements, satisfying your inner purpose? Choice is yours. But I would rather tell you, let us dive into the infinite possibilities of your subconscious and enjoy this divine blessing with a peaceful heart every night, allowing your subconscious to choose everything for you in a divinely guided way and wake up in joy in order to greet the world, saying:

Yes, here I am with all my essence, with all that divine grace that I have within since the primordial time of my existence. Thanks to the world. Thanks to those divine blessings. Thanks to the infinite universal intelligence. Thanks for being with me. Thanks for sheltering me and for making me believe that I, too, have a special purpose on this earth… and here I am, not only for a mortal existence but also for a spiritual journey instead.

21 | Meditation: A Gateway to Feel Your Spiritual Being

"I did not even know where I was going. For the first few hours, it was complete darkness, and it seemed to me that I was quite in a state of oblivion, yet descending down, down into the darkness, into that depth more and more, maybe, in order to explore a mystery, I felt! But the more I descended, the more I felt that I was being guided up by a tiny flame of light within, and trust me, the deeper I plunged into that darkness, the more I started to feel that I was not there only to confront that darkness all around me. Rather, there had been a vast sea of eternal, graceful light to embrace, and that tiny flame of light was just guiding me up towards that eternal light, towards that ocean of grace and bliss, and I was just walking through it, and that tiny flame was leading me up all through my sojourn only to be merged with that eternal vastness, where there is no darkness at all, but only a vast sea of graceful light.

Then I did not even know what meditation is, what the exact process is to experience that harmony and bliss within. But that day, something happened that made me startle with awe and wonder! After that experience, I started to feel that beyond this mortal realm of human existence, I do have another reality, another existence. And that reality is not the tangibility we see with the help of our ordinary perceptions, but rather the reality that holds the truth of eternity; the truth of an eternal bliss that we have within since the primordial time of our existence."

She paused for a while, and then continued:

"You may be surprised a bit! But trust me dear, at that very moment, I was not in me, to put it right, I was beyond any realm of tangibility, beyond any realm of conscious or subconscious, but I was there with my true essence, with my entity, very much aligned with the divinity within; very much true to my eternal existence and connected to that supreme power of divine intelligence!"

You may be perplexed a bit, may think, was it really a state of meditation for her or something else that cannot be comprehended in the tangible realm of perception? If you think so and are not been able to perceive the matter in a deeper sense, I would rather assure you that it was truly a state of meditation for that lady when her inner quietude became more realistic in a self-reflective way and the infinite potentials of her soul became rejuvenated once again to embrace that eternal divine grace (that surrounded the entire universe and her entity as well). And I feel it is the very moment of being able to feel one's divinity within. It is the ideal way to perceive the bliss and serenity, the truth and integrity of one's inner self, that most of the time we fail to contemplate in our day-to-day life of broken promises and unattainable hopes!

In this connection, once again I would like to remind you, if we consider our life as a journey itself, it would be better for us to value our life as a spiritual quest and meditation as the heart and soul of this spiritual journey not only to communicate with ourselves, to know the true purpose of our being, but also to communicate with the world outside, to heal the wounds (not only for us but for others as well) and to restore ourselves physically, mentally and spiritually as well.

And this same case held true for that lady whom I met five years ago at a less renowned ashram in the northern region of India. She had been a disciple over there for the last few years. And it was one of her experiences during the time of meditation that she shared with me. I feel you are pretty curious to know whether she was a nun (a 'sanyasini' in that sense) or not. So, to satisfy your curiosity, I would like to tell you that she was not like that; rather, an ordinary woman of barely forty to forty-two years of age.

And here, once again I would like to remind you that meditation is not only for the yogis but for all, especially for those who have been distracted from their ideal path of truth and reality and are suffering from an existential crisis like that lady who, throughout her life of suffering, ultimately realised that her soul needed proper healing and that could not be done without the help of meditation. It not only gave her that healing but also introduced her to a different reality of her existence. In this connection, once again I would like to tell you that it is not only a scientific process advocated by psychologists but also acts as an antidote to eradicate all forms of wounds in order to have a greater insight, to know the real nature of yourself and to awaken your soul to that eternal truth of harmony and bliss.

When Meditation Helps to Ground Yourself with Your True Being

If some of you are feeling that our human life is nothing but only a confinement to face several unbroken chains of miseries and sorrows where happiness cannot be perceived, cannot be embraced, I would like to remind you one simple fact that in spite of all the sufferings and miseries, you can also have bliss within. And herein lies the secret of meditation that always helps you to open up your heart, allowing your soul to feel that bliss, that serenity, within. During the course of this blissful practice, you may realise where the actual worth of surrendering yourself completely to the divine lies.

What you need to do is just to meditate with a peaceful mind and with a thankful heart. Yes! It has that magical power to transcend your consciousness beyond this tangible realm of sorrows and sufferings, enabling your heart and rejuvenating your soul once again to bring alchemy into the gross realities of your mundane life.

And herein lies the efficacy of transmuting one's ordinary life into a life of blissful truth and harmony. In this connection, one more fact that I would like to share with you. Some of you may feel that meditation is only for spiritual persons. At this point, I must tell you that meditation is not only a spiritual exploration, but it is also a scientific art at the same time. Hence, it is for everyone. Whether you believe in God or not, you cannot deny that you are a spiritual being, a soul with an earthly shell. Yoga and meditation are universal, as they have that infinite potential of strengthening your energy and channelizing your spirit to recognise your worth, your true purpose on this planet. It enables you to eradicate all forms of dilemmas and helps you to join all your fragmented thoughts into one simple harmonious accord, inspiring you once again to move forward in your life.

If being awakened to your soul's purpose seems to you as some sweet fragrance of the morning buds, remember meditation is that special moment of a newer dawn to enrich their fragrance, helping them to bloom once again with all those inherent potentials they have within since eternity.

While you are considering your life as a spiritual quest, meditation can be considered as that magical stone that will help you all the time to feel this quest not as a tough one, but a blissful sojourn in order to come back to your centre, avoiding all forms of distractions and leading your consciousness towards a higher level of contemplation where you will be able to free yourself from all forms of illusive expectations through an insightful realisation and also can feel the highest truth of life and that blissful divinity you have within since eternity.

Meditation is nothing but to explore your divinity once again in spite of living in this mortal realm of existence, unfolding another truth of your existence where the concept of 'I', your ego self, gets faded away and quite automatically you start to feel that you are getting invited into a state of blissful silence in order to be aligned with the reality of your spiritual being. And herein lies its magical power, making you realise that you have a hidden truth under the layer of your mortal existence. And that truth is nothing but the truth of your spiritual essence, the truth of eternity itself.

Though meditation does not have any specific process, it is all about grounding yourself, coming back to the depth within that still seems to us an unfathomable mystery. It is all about feeling, experiencing and transcending beyond this tangible realm, uplifting our consciousness and introducing ourselves to the truth within our entity. It is meditation that awakens us to the experience of who we truly are and what our purpose on this earth is. Here, we do not need any special arrangement or method to connect to the divine, as meditation does not require special preparation, but always requires an intense urge to feel the connection with the higher source of intelligence. It is also a journey where your body, mind and soul are integrated in a harmonious way, and you can feel that you are treading along a blissful path, only to know your inner self and your connection to the divine.

But do you ever know how it is possible to evolve yourself while being grounded in your true being at the same time? Here lies the mystery of this art. Yes, it is an art, an art of channelizing your mind in a concentrated way while at the same time elevating your consciousness beyond this tangible realm of perception. Though meditation always requires a properly concentrated mind, never think that this concentration alone is enough to bring that divinity within. Concentration means one-pointedness of thought, and meditation is delving into the depth of your being through a concentrated mind to bring balance within, guiding your consciousness in a constructively fruitful way so that you can realise the truth of life itself—the reality of your inner world.

And here lies its distinction from concentration, its difference from an ordinary prayer. A faithful prayer also acts as a bridge between your conscious and subconscious self, and it can also bring a miracle into your life, but meditation is something higher. And remember, during that moment, you are not only elevating your concentrated energy towards a fruitful exploration, but also rejuvenating your soul's intense yearning once again to be reconnected to the divine, to that supreme power of intelligence surrounding the universe since eternity.

To put it simply, meditation is nothing but a reunion of your soul with that greater womb of creation from where she came and into which she will be merged. So, whenever you feel bereaved, wandering and stumbling across the darkest corners of reality, never be disheartened. Rather, pause for a while and feel free to contemplate. Never force yourself to do so. Instead, try to detach yourself from worldly distractions in a spontaneous way. Still, some thoughts and memories, happy or unhappy, may pop into your mind. You may feel you are getting distracted again, but don't get bothered. Instead try to descend more into the depths within, surpassing the limitations and distractions of your conscious self. The dark passageways of tangible realities may distract you for a while, but try to ignore their call and listen to what your inner self is whispering into your ears. And I am sure there, once again, you may feel that strong yearning of your soul that wants to be merged with the divine light, with that supreme power of intelligence.

In this connection, I would like to remind you that meditation is essential not only to be psychologically balanced, but also to maintain your integrity as a spiritual being. If meditation is the heart and soul of your spiritual life, your mind has to be considered as the principal instrument to continue that life.

Though there are always different opinions regarding these paths of meditation, there are multiple opinions and multiple ways to connect to the divine. But the first and foremost way to this connection is to calm your mind and allow it to follow the path of the truth that you have been seeking for a long time. There is no formality on this path, but if you are able to attain it, trust me, you may find yourself in a state of sublime bliss. There, you need not be baffled or wander around like a hopeless tramp; rather, you may realise where lies the mystery of your existence, the truth of your being. You can even explore the eternal knot that you share with that universal divine source of intelligence. And quite surprisingly, all the thoughts of worries and sorrows gradually start to fade away, and once again you may feel that you are an eternal source of energy and that your purpose on this earth is not to mourn over past griefs, but to contemplate, observe and feel the bliss within, instead of seeking it from the external world.

There is no formality in attaining this path, but one thing we must remember is that it is neither a tough nor an easy one to undergo. Even the mystics and yogis sometimes fail to attain it. It takes time. It is a long process; an art of exploration indeed, exploring yourself, exploring the spiritual essence that you have within since eternity. And here lies its truth, its wonder.

Meditation: An Integrated and Blissful Experience of Body, Mind and Soul

Though there is no specific process regarding this art of meditation, to connect ourselves completely to the divine in order to elevate our consciousness beyond this tangible realm of perception, we need to maintain a proper balance within. It may help us to become more enlightened in a spontaneous and constructive way. Though there are several opinions and principles regarding this art of meditation, there is also a general principle that embodies the universal truth, and that truth is nothing but the truth of controlling your mind and elevating your consciousness in that way, from where you can feel your spiritual essence within yourself and your eternal connection with the divine as well. Here, in this section, I would like to give you some of the disciplines that may lead your consciousness to feel that harmony and bliss within once again:

- Since meditation is a harmonious practice of mind, body and soul, in order to attain that highest sublime bliss, along with a thankful heart and a peaceful mind, you also need to have a healthy body. During this course of meditation, a comfortable, steady posture is essential to calm your mind, relax your nerves, and feel more connected to the divine with an open heart. A steady but comfortable posture not only helps you maintain your mental equilibrium but also enables you to concentrate more on a specific thought and contemplate it in a spontaneously peaceful way. Your insight becomes clearer, and gradually, you start to feel that you are aligning yourself with your divinity within.
- Next comes the discipline of breathing, as it is closely connected to our life force. So, proper breathing is essential for healing and for feeling your connection with the eternal forces of nature. Proper breathing (breathe in and breathe out) not only helps you eradicate all forms of worry and tension, but also gives you the strength to reground yourself within your centre, helping you gain greater insight and enabling you to broaden your vision systematically.
- But I think this breathing (this rhythmic pattern of breathing in and breathing out) has to be learned under some supervision, as it is very much a scientific practice. Hence it is not advisable to do it in a haphazard manner. If it is done in an improper way, it may create an imbalance not only in your mind but also in your body.
- Cleanliness of your body and purity of your heart and mind are essential to feel the blissful reality of your life through meditation. With an impure heart and a restless mind, you can never devote yourself to the divine. It will always hold you back, withdrawing you once again from surrendering yourself to the divine in a spontaneous way.

- In this connection, I would remind you that our mind is very much insolent in nature, and it is also an art to learn how to bring that unruly mind completely under your own control. Actually, meditation is all about controlling your scattered mind at one time in a harmonious, constructive way, withdrawing your sense organs from all forms of worldly distractions and fixing your mind on one simple thought without interruption, without any forceful external intrusion, and without any contradictions. It is that state of your mind when your internal stream keeps flowing without any interferences.
- To put it in a more comprehensible way, meditation is that state of your mind when, within yourself, you may not find any objective consciousness to perceive your tangible existence. But that does not mean that there is no consciousness at all. There is a consciousness, indeed, a pure consciousness, the subjective one, which is more to interpret a state of bliss and solitude where you are with your real nature, with the truth of your existence that you have within you since eternity.
- If you think meditation is only a simple process of concentrating and controlling your mind to bring balance to your personality, I would say that, apart from that, it also serves a special role in your life. And that is bringing integrity within your being. And here meditation is serving that purpose, to get yourself reunited with your original centre, the truth of your being that you have lost in the course of your everyday life.
- In a deeper state of meditation, you will be able to elevate your consciousness beyond any level of tangible perception, beyond all forms of worries and anxieties. It is that stage when your soul, breaking the shackles of ignorance, finds her own way to realign herself with the supreme power of universal intelligence, with her true

home, the home of infinite potentials and unperturbed bliss. In a way, meditation is to be considered a blessing in this spiritual journey we are embarked on, as with the help of it, quite automatically, the unifying, constructive undercurrent of your inner self starts to flow within in a harmonious way and, quite surprisingly, starts to channelize its energy even on the external layer of your mind, enabling you to restore your inner balance and helping you to communicate not only with yourself but also with the world outside in a proper way, eradicating all forms of inner conflicts and dilemmas and opening up a newer insight to perceive the world with a newer vision of reality.

Some of you may think that it is only a spiritual process and only the yogis can attain this path with long perseverance. But here, I would like to remind you that it is not only a spiritual process but also a scientific process, indeed, advocated by most psychologists to heal their patients, where the patients themselves can explore their reality and ground themselves in their true being with the help of this artful discovery. Knowing ourselves, our soul's nature and responding to her call is the actual knowledge, and herein lies the realignment of our being with the truth of our existence; herein lies the efficacy of meditation, the art of discovering yourself.

It Always Invites You towards a State of Self- Reflection

In this life, we are all seeking something — something that may embrace us with joy and happiness, totally forgetting that the actual secret of being happy forever lies therein. Actually, we are all spiritual beings in mortal forms, and that is why our essential nature lies beyond this tangible realm of worldly perceptions.

But most of the time, we engage ourselves in the trap of this mundane reality and ignore the reality of our being, the inherent core of our existence that we have within, since eternity. And I feel meditation is nothing but a systematic and scientific practice to uplift our consciousness from that level of ignorance in a self-reflective way, making us realise that our human life is not only to seek pleasures and happiness in the external world, but also to discover that bliss and serenity within, that remained unexplored due to our mere ignorance.

During the deeper state of meditation, you can perceive the ultimate reality of your inner self, the truth you bear since eternity within your entity. But it is possible only when your mind is calm enough. Then only you can feel that this meditative state is nothing but a mirror itself to behold your real nature in front of you. And gradually you start to feel that you are no longer an earthly body, but a soul with a human form. And this world of earthly belongings, your name, your fame and all other worldly things are nothing but illusive things to be lulled on.

If we consider our mind as an ocean and the waves hitting the shore as the regular thoughts that come into our minds (sometimes intentionally and sometimes unintentionally), I would rather remind you that meditation is a helpful guide for exploring the depths of that ocean. And there you may not find any ripples, any constraints or any bubbles of thoughts coming to and fro, but only can feel the sublimity, the serenity and peace, inviting you into a world of harmony and bliss. During this meditative state, you may not perceive your real being at first, but if you probe deeper within, you can feel the magic, you can hear the soft mumblings of your soul and what she is sharing with you, even in the midst of that silence around you. Here, in this deeper stage of meditation, you can no longer feel any restraint from your ego self, rather may start to feel that you are opening up a newer door to liberate your soul from all the barriers and bondages of this tangible world, true to her real essence in order to be merged with the supreme power of intelligence from where she came into this mundane world of existence.

And coming to this point of experience, you can only realise wherein lies the secret of feeling the bliss within, the secret of feeling happy while your external scenarios are not even permitting you to do so. Some of you may doubt the entire process, may not perceive its utility in your life, with the help of your ordinary consciousness. But my dear, if you allow your consciousness to broaden its horizon, I can assure you that there you may have a greater insight through this self-reflective way, where this self-reflection ultimately will prove a revelation itself. A revelation of the higher truth, the truth of your existence as well.

When Purification Happens, Enlightenment Comes in a Spontaneous Way

Do you ever know what the real purpose of meditation is? Is it only calming your mind or integrating it in a harmonious way? Or something else, something beyond our ordinary perceptions? To put it in a simplistic way, I would rather say that the meditative stage is that purified state of our mind when we are totally free from all forms of negative emotions and thoughts and can engage ourselves only in quest of the ideal truth, in order to explore our true spiritual nature and to be enlightened with the eternal light to feel the divinity once again, that we already have within.

If you want to be spiritually enlightened, always remember that purification of your mind and heart and enlightenment of your soul is inextricably connected to each other. It is utterly impossible for you to reach that greater height of pure enlightenment unless and until you are fully able to free yourself from all forms of negative and lower vibrational energies surrounding you. Sometimes you yourself are responsible for welcoming those, and sometimes circumstances bring those unwanted vibrations close to you.

So always try to keep in your mind that whenever you are going to attain the path of meditation, you need to be very free from all the toxicities of your surroundings. A toxic, impure mind can never attain that highest path of the universal source of intelligence. Purification of your mind not only frees you from all forms of toxicities and negativities, but also enlivens your soul once again in order to reach that highest order from where you can get the knowledge of self-realisation. And this self-realisation is the ultimate way to ground your being and elevate your consciousness at the same time, to enlighten your being and to emerge before the world as a truly balanced and enlightened individual who knows how to feel the bliss within, despite living in this mundane world of existence.

In a way, it also provides you with a greater insight to comprehend yourself and the world outside in a more cognitive way. And herein lies its ability to provide you with a better, intelligent understanding to recognise your true purpose on this planet and your relation to it.

Knowing Your Spiritual Worth Is the Ideal Way to Heal Yourself

Most of you may feel that on this planet, your existence does not have any meaning at all. Here, you have to face different circumstances in different scenarios all the time. Sometimes favourable, sometimes not. Most of the time, you feel a lack inside. Your conscious self every time harks you back. Sometimes it tempts you to enjoy some worldly things to fill in that lack. But most of the time, you fail to do so and discover yourself once again trapped in another labyrinthine pleasure-seeking track where, once again, you find nothing but that same lack!

Do you ever know why, again and again, you feel the same lack, in spite of having everything around you? I think you do not know the answer. And herein lies your ignorance. Actually, that lack is not coming from the external world, but it is coming from your inner self. Nowadays, the more you are getting attached to external worldly pleasures, the more you are ignoring the truth that you are a spiritual being and on this planet, you also have some destined purpose. And herein lies the root cause of that lack you are feeling every hour of your survival. In this connection, one more thing that I would like to share is that most often we tend to see our existence as mere survival, while the truth is something higher than that, something very much aligned with the truth of the universe that we already have within, since eternity.

I feel suffering in our physical plane and experiencing that lack within is nothing but one of the real consequences of our spiritual deprivation. And this process of meditation is nothing but to realign ourselves with our true home, strengthening our spirit, healing our wounds, bringing before us the real nature of ourselves and allowing our soul to evolve once again, true to her own essence. In a deeper way to interpret, meditation is that state of your mind when the depth can only speak with the depth and open up all the doors of perceptions to allow your consciousness to transcend beyond the ordinary level of perceptions, beyond all the sufferings, beyond all the tangibility that is harking you back every now and then.

And the moment you encounter your true spiritual self, quite automatically, you get to know who you truly are and from where you came into this world of existence. And gradually you start to feel that here on this earth you are not a single entity, but eternally connected to the supreme power of universal intelligence, surrounding the entire creation and responsible for your existence as well. So, you don't need to be frightened or depressed by anything external, as you are already complete within. And while you are already complete within, you need not lend something external to make yourself happy. And now you are already aware of who you truly are. You know your spiritual worth; your eternal self, the truth of your being, the Absolute Reality that you possess within since the time of your primordial existence. And the moment you start to accept who you truly are, quite automatically, you will be able to heal yourself and evolve within. As acceptance can bring within you that feeling of bliss your soul has been searching for a long time. And quite automatically, you start to feel that the cause of your depression was nothing but an estrangement from your inner seed, your centre, your reality within.

I personally feel that meditation is a blessing for both of our psychological and spiritual well-being. Actually, this is a moment of revelation; a revelation of the truth of our being, a revelation of our real self; the infinite power and eternal strength that we all have within our entity.

This is that precious state of our mind when we realise that we do not have any beginning or any end. We do not have any particular place. We do not have any colour, nor do we have any shape. Rather, we are eternal. We are souls in a mortal frame.

Yes, it is a wonder to have that feeling within. And meditation can make this wonder happen in your real state of existence, that state of existence where you cannot distinguish yourself from this universal source of energy, but can identify yourself everywhere with that. And this is the highest form of wisdom that a true meditator can attain. And herein lies the true worth of meditation, where self-realisation is the only keyword to elevate your mind, balance yourself and enlighten your soul with the grace of harmony, truth and eternity.

22 | Let Your Soul Be Your Foster Mother

"It seemed like a dark tunnel I was walking through! There was no one to hold my hand, no one to talk with, but deep within, I heard a voice though mumbling it had been, but I was sure enough that it had been that special voice that could help me to overcome that dark tunnel all through ever, and trust me, it was not only a voice indeed, but a sparkling candle I felt to enlighten me towards that path of Truth, towards that path of divine consciousness from where I came and will be merged into."

She paused for a while, and then continued:

"At that very moment, I did not know whose voice that was, but deep within, I was sure of the fact that she was no one but must be my foster mother, for whom I still have this existence, this precious existence that continually reminds me of who I am. Do you want to know who my foster mother is?"

She said nothing, but closed her eyes. Tears rolled down her cheeks, and she gazed at the evening sky, maybe to feel the tranquillity, maybe to feel that essence within her she has, since the day of eternity. Then she said:

"She is no one, my dear; she is my ideal friend, my guide; my Soul indeed!"

The stars kept smiling overhead. The wind was blowing in its natural way. On that day I could not ask her anything further, but only chose to feel the serenity within, much like her.

Actually, during those days, I was at Pondicherry for fifteen days where, quite fortunately, I met her during one of my beach walks in the morning. And within a few days, just through a few short conversations, I started to feel that she, too, had a voice like me. We started meeting at regular intervals and, quite unknowingly to her, during one of those regular beach walks, she confessed a hidden truth about her life: the truth of choosing the life of a simple painter, negating her so-called successful life as a highly paid engineer! Yes! This was the truth of her existence; the truth of her soul's voice indeed!

Let's Contemplate Within and Feel Your Soul Once Again

You may be a bit surprised, or you may even feel how it is possible for a lady aged between forty and forty-five to leave her job altogether and choose the path of her soul's calling? Is it really wise to make this decision at this age? Or is it nothing but only an irresponsible approach to life? If these questions are coming into your mind and asking you to think in a rational way, I would rather remind you at this stage that our soul has nothing to do with a linear, logical pattern. Rather, she has her own voice, her own rhythm, her own vitality and reality indeed! Yes! And herein lies her magic itself!

In a deeper way to interpret, our soul is that invisible pearl within our entity, that inner space of our consciousness that is continually guiding us to behold our reflection, continually helping us to perceive who we are in reality. It is not a thing to be touched, but an essence to be felt within; an essence to feel the depth of your being, transcending your consciousness towards the path of divine intelligence. In a way, it is that greater womb from where you have come into your earthly existence and where you will be merged into after this mortal life. And the more you delve within your unconscious, the more you can feel the infinite power and abundant possibilities lurking beneath the depth of your psyche, the more you can feel wherein lies your true calling, wherein lies the true meaning of your existence.

A question may hinder your mind:

"Who am I? Am I only a mortal body grovelling over this earth with all my mortal existence? Or am I an invisible entity, intensely alive with all my presence?"

But if you probe more into your unconscious in a deeper way, you can feel wherein that limitless dimension of eternity lies. There, you cannot feel the borderline between your inner and outer experience. Then only your soul will open up towards the magic of that Infinite truth, and quite spontaneously, your ordinary consciousness may start to transcend itself towards that path of universal intelligence. And herein lies the miraculous power of your soul, the transcendental reality of your existence as well, where being grounded with your centre is nothing but an opportunity to evolve yourself. And the moment when every perception of your inner experience starts to flow in a natural way, you can quite automatically feel wherein the true purpose of your existence lies.

And I feel that the more you probe your unconscious, the more you will align with your inner purpose; the more you will be awakened to the truth of that universal intelligence from which you came and to which you will be merged. Contemplating within and perceiving that inner purpose is simply feeling your divine presence once again and aligning with your soul's purpose.

I still remember those last words of that lady: *"Actually, that night came to me as some sort of revelation… a blessing perhaps! And all of a sudden, I realised that here I am for a special reason. I just closed my eyes and, quite spontaneously, the wilderness of that nocturnal beauty started to paint herself with a newer brush, on a newer canvas. I did not know how, but it happened, and deep within my heart I started to feel that the entire universe was trying to whisper into my ears and asking me to be in my real essence!"*

Yes! A revelation, a blessing, it was that ultimately helped her paint the wilderness of that night on her canvas, not only to explore the hidden artistic self, lurking beneath her but also to respond to her soul's calling that had been continually harking her back to ground herself in her true centre. A soul's calling is nothing but another form of homecoming, where your entity finds the eternal solace that it was searching for over a long period.

And the more you probe deep into your unconscious, the more you will get aligned with that special type of consciousness, and the more you can feel that place where your soul resides. And herein lies the magic itself, the magic of an altered state of consciousness where our soul is open and we are able enough to perceive the true meaning of our life, our existence as well.

Let's Channelize Your Consciousness towards the Truth of Divine Intelligence in a Spontaneous Way

Though in a linear, logical way of understanding, surrendering to your soul's choice may appear before the world as something unrealistic, the more you probe deeper into your unconscious, the more you can realise wherein lies the actual truth, beyond the temporal, beyond the physical, beyond the mundane. And the moment you get aligned with that inner truth, quite spontaneously your sole purpose will come to the fore and you'll realise that you've a spiritual existence, more than this mundane body.

Contemplating within, perceiving the real meaning of your existence and surrendering your entity to your soul's choice is not only going through a psycho-spiritual journey, but also preserving within that ultimate truth of universal intelligence. As I feel, the moment we get detached from our soul's calling, we actually get detached not only from our centre, but also from our ideal purpose and consequently get ourselves stuck in this labyrinthine spell of meaninglessness, once again.

Surrendering to your soul's choice is nothing but to feel your inner experience once again and emerge before the world with your real nature, strengthening your intuitive self and discovering that eternal accord with which you need to be grounded. Yes, it has been the centre of your being and coming back to this centre is nothing but cleansing the doors of perception, getting aligned with that higher purpose of existence and reconciling with that universal power of divine intelligence in order to restore the balance within.

Surrendering to Your Soul's Call Has the Power to Heal Your Entity as Never Before

At first, this surrender may create some incongruence within your entity. You may start to feel some gaps, some lacks between your outer and inner experiences. But gradually you start to realise where the difference lies. You start to feel that this surrender surely has a different meaning within, a special purpose not only to enlighten you to the truth of that divine intelligence, but also to evolve your entity entirely in a new direction; a direction of true emergence.

Quite gradually, you start to realise that your ordinary consciousness is getting aligned with a special type of consciousness, and there you don't need to be conscious of what is actually going on around the outer sphere of perception. But deep within, you can feel that your inner quietude is perceiving that experience in silence. And quite spontaneously, you'll start to realise wherein exactly lies your soul's power of true emergence; wherein lies the true power of becoming what your soul prefers you to be. And in this state of consciousness, gradually you'll get more attuned to the spiritual dimension of your existence, being in full harmony with the divine essence within yourself.

And trust me; the more you surrender yourself to your soul's calling, the more you start to heal your heart not only by strengthening your centre once again, but also by bringing yourself back to your ultimate root of existence. And the more you get awakened and enlightened to the universal truth of your spiritual existence, the more you start to explore wherein lies the actual mystery of life itself. Moreover, surrendering to your soul's calling not only helps you to emerge before the world in your real essence but also guides you to be anchored to your own essence, true to your being.

But most of the time, to fit ourselves into this so-called parameter of success and progression, we tend to forget our soul's calling and, consequently, fall into the trap of incongruence and the related depression. And the more we get disconnected from this soul's calling, the more we get frustrated, and as a result of that, we're not only separated from our ground of being, but also fail to discover the truth of our existence as well. Being grounded within our being is nothing but reconciliation with the divine force that we already have within, since the time of eternity.

So, in a simpler way to interpret, surrendering to your soul's choice is nothing but accepting who you truly are and being an individual candle of your own authentic self. And this not only builds your foundation once again, but also transforms your depressed self into a newer one where the dark, pitchy clouds of suffering quite automatically paint themselves with some newer, vibrant colours in a newer rhythm, and once again, you start to feel that you too have a special existence. Moreover, you start to feel that you're not only a mundane body, but also a spiritual being with an eternal existence. And it is possible only when you'll be able to feel your soul's voice within, wherein lies the grace of truth and eternity.

In this connection, I would remind you of another fact, i.e. the painting on that reflective night came to that lady as a canvas itself, I feel. And there, only her soul could find that brush to paint herself in a newer way. There, you cannot find any logical linearity or any rational understanding of it. But there, the Art itself spoke of its aliveness, spoke of its eternal beauty, grace and truth. And herein lies the magic itself, the magic of healing one's heart, the magic of perceiving the truth of eternity; the magic of our Being, our existence as well.

That painting was not only a painting to behold the beauty of that night, but it was something special that was very much connected to her soul's yearning. And it was all because of her soul, she ultimately succeeded in discovering her centre once again and in emerging before the world in her true essence.

Remember, You're Not Alone, But Your Soul Is Always with You

Surrendering to your soul's choice is not only choosing your inner experiences as the ideal form of realisation, but also preserving harmony within and guiding your unconscious in a way to create something out of nothing.

Actually, in this modern cybernetic civilisation, quite often we fail to find our ideal purpose. And this failure can also be considered as one of the deprivations at the spiritual level. Our souls yearn for something, but we run after something else without properly knowing what our ideal purpose in this world of existence is. Every time, we run after something. Yes! An endless run it has been, but we never find that ideal purpose for which we're born.

But a complete surrender to our soul allows our entity to flourish in a newer way and invites our heart once again to speak with depth. As a complete and honest surrender to your soul's choice, it is nothing but ascending your entity towards the highest truth of universal intelligence and evolving yourself once again into a self-reflective journey in a fruitful and constructive way.

"The painting on that blessed night was neither an escape nor a confinement to me; it came to me all along as reconciliation, as something very much akin to my heart."

That lady said gently and closed her eyes in deep serenity. Truly, herein lies the magic of surrendering yourself to your soul's choice, surrendering yourself to the enigmatic life force that you've had within, since eternity. There, you may not get that much material prosperity to be fitted into this so-called society of progression and success, but there, you can feel that divine grace within to behold yourself in a newer way, in spite of all the negativities surrounding your life. As our soul is only that phoenix itself to ground our entity with its ideal purpose, it gives us that faith and power to endure all kinds of sufferings and gently whispers into our ears:

"Come on, get up, my dear! Life is not to mourn over, but to dance, believe and explore your potential...and to feel yourself worthy enough!"

On that very evening, nothing happened that much. But both of us preferred to close our eyes. And deep within my heart, I somehow felt that my inner experience was getting aligned with an enigmatic force surrounding the entire universe. I didn't know why, but I felt it like a bliss; a guidance, perhaps, that was coming deep within, much like my soul's heritage, I felt. Much like my mother, my home to reconcile with!

23 | Let's Find the Home You're Destined for

"I was vigorously in search of something. It was a dark wood. I was moving faster. It seemed that the mountain was very much close to me where I needed to take shelter for that night. Those labyrinthine ups and downs of that hilly road were quite hazardous and unpredictable as well. Somehow, I felt that I was searching for my home that had been lost for some decades…

I was climbing upwards, finding no valley to take some rest. I was very eager to reach at my long-awaited destination. Sometimes I thought it might be around that dark wood. Sometimes I went on faster, thinking that I might find that on that mountain top. I was moving and moving. A dark night it was. But I did not care at all. I was simply drawn towards something, but suddenly, some mysterious energy jerked me at once in a miraculous way! That dark night suddenly went off, leaving me once again in the midst of that wood, only to feel that the eastern sky was getting scarlet again. I felt that the mountain was as far from me as before. And still, I was at that same place. So, what was I searching for? I did not find that answer. But for some unknown reason, I felt very much happy within. Tears came into my eyes. I felt it like a home, an eternal abode of bliss and shelter!

This was only an expression of a writer whom I met during my visit to Manali. It just came up in the way of a casual conversation that we used to have at a roadside cafeteria. He used to share his experiences during creative crisis, which, more or less, we all have during non-creative hours when we rigorously try to engage ourselves in creating something special. In those days, he was trying to portray the adventurous life of an archaeologist who had lost his way altogether and, in a dejected mood, trying to figure out the best way, back to his home. And it was in the course of writing that situation that writer himself had such a dream of losing his own home, and it was only that experience he shared with me on that afternoon.

When Transcendental Consciousness Leads You to Find Your Higher Calling

I feel you are eager enough to know where that archaeologist was trying to reach. Is it the same place that the writer also longed for in his own life? If you have this intuitive feeling, I would rather say that you are absolutely right, my dear.

Sometimes in your life, you may feel lost, with no clear path to your next destination. At that very moment, I would rather tell you never get bothered, try to peep into your inner land. There you may find some mesmerising answers. Though your logical mind may not validate those solutions, if you allow your consciousness to expand its horizon, you may perceive that there is another kingdom outside your known territory, beyond the reach of this tangible world, very precious and intangibly creative.

Some of you may feel that the actual home always needs to be built in a meticulous way with minute effort and diligence on a solid ground of the material plane. However, I will not dishearten those of you who prefer to build this kind of home, as there is nothing wrong in achieving such material goals.

But have you ever felt any lack, despite achieving all this material success? If so, let me tell you that this lack is nothing but, on the other hand, it is trying to engage you to explore something different. It is nothing but a spiritual quest I feel, in order to search for your ideal destination, your true purpose on this planet. And it is only through this spiritual quest that you may discover the deeper meaning of your higher calling — A call to realign yourself with your higher self — A call that is seemingly lost but buried deep inside your entity. And I feel this call can only be answered if you reconnect your soul, that eternal flowing fountain of your entity, to that universal divine energy, if not in a tangible way, then in a way of transcendental consciousness that always inspires you to believe in the existence of an unseen territory that continually prepares you to a higher purpose you are destined for, beyond this tangible world of material progression.

Such was the case of that writer. Frankly speaking, he was also struggling with that same crisis. Though, to some extent, it is right to interpret that in a creative crisis, on a deeper level, that was something different, which is why that night he had that unexpected dream. Some of you may think it was only a symbolic expression of his storyline that came into his dream, a way to release his thoughts; the search of an archaeologist who had lost his way back to his home.

Though it may be true on an apparent level, if you fathom deep into it, you may have a different realisation. You may also feel that the writer was on a journey, on a quest to explore himself. He was also searching for a special connection to his home that had been lost for a long time, he felt. This was the reason that his higher self was screaming inside, continually reminding him of his true purpose. That dream was nothing but an image of his subconscious search for an ideal home.

Quite unexpectedly, while he was having that dream, he suddenly felt a special energy that was about to fill his entity. He did not know where it came from, but he felt it like an eternal home. It may startle you; you may feel, 'How is it possible?' As in his dream, he had not reached his destination. So, what made him feel so happy and content? Here at this juncture lies the mystery itself. But let me tell you one thing. You may be surprised to know that we are all on the same page, searching for our destination, but never finding that ideal one. As a result, we are getting frustrated but never allowing ourselves to lay bare the mystery hidden at the core of our being—the address of our ideal home since the primordial time of our existence.

Yearning for the HOME Is the Only Way to Find Peace and Liberation

While you're climbing up the happy stairs of your life, usually you don't have that much need or time to look back or pause for a while. Then you are just moving on. Then, you've got everything to make you feel satisfied. So, on an apparent level, there is no need to think about it deeply. During this phase of gaining material prosperity, the undercurrent of your ego always pushes you forward, and as a result of that, your Survival self has nothing to do but to be a slave at his hand. And at the same time, you may feel unhappy inside, and a deep sense of conflict starts to brim over your Intermediary self. In spite of all the material luxuries, a sense of lack, a sense of losing your shelter, may begin to grow within, leading to the loss of your centre —the guiding principle of your existence.

In the very first place, while your Inner Mind prepares you to have this realisation, you may feel perturbed a bit and a deeper sense of hopelessness unexpectedly starts to pervade your entity. You may feel your entire foundation is not stable enough. As a result of that, a sense of uncertainty and the related existential crisis may start to create bubbles of boredom and anxiety within yourself. This is also the cause of an unexplained dilemma that you may face for a while on the layer of your external conscious mind. You may start to feel your entire existence is crumbling down. You've nowhere to go, and your craving for that ideal destination is nothing but an elusive image to wander around. And here, at this juncture, your inner self may put forth a question before you:

"Is it the right Home I'm destined for?"

You may pause for a moment, but from then on, quite unexpectedly, your ideal journey begins once again for a different search, for an ideal Home.

For some days, you may wander around thinking, 'Why is this happening?' While you've got everything to sustain, so why are you feeling this lack? The questions may come around like swirling mists, blurring your vision and leaving you, once again, hopeless with all your existential despair. But I would suggest you, my dear, do not get disheartened. Maybe you are just on a journey to find out that eternal peace your soul has been longing for. Maybe in the course of gaining material prosperity, somehow, you've neglected your soul's desire, the prime life force of your being. And here, this sense of homelessness you're experiencing is nothing but a feeling of losing that centre and the deepest urge of realigning yourself with your true home, that eternal abode of shelter and security.

In a way, it is nothing but a spiritual quest to recognise your true being, allowing your spirit once again to make you feel not as a single entity but to feel the harmony, the wholeness within. Then all the conflicts will start to blur automatically. And you may start to feel the presence of that ideal destination within the core of your being, nowhere else, nowhere outside. Your face will rejoice again with a surprising divine satisfaction.

Once again, you may start to feel you're complete and content, liberated even in this mortal realm, and truly connected to your dream destination: the house of eternity and bliss.

Nurturing a Garden to Feel the Presence of Your Home

In order to mingle your being with that stream of harmony, you need to open up your heart's desire so that your soul can play her flute of eternity without any hindrance. If you listen to her song, your mind will naturally lead you to a different state of consciousness, where this song of homecoming may fill your being once again with a sense of celebration —a celebration of your heart's desire, a celebration for that destination you are waiting for. And through her song, a deeper realisation may come, quite unexpectedly, like a sudden flash of lightning. From then on, you may start to perceive that eternal cord you have with her. You may hear her voice coming from the deepest corner of your own entity:

"A thousand times you came.
A thousand times you will be back,
Is it really a puzzle to solve?
Or another destination to halt?
Hope you are ready enough to wrap up your tiny packsack
To find out that place that may fill you up once again
With that beauty inside, with that much-awaited grace!"

So now it is time to behold yourself, not within the tiny framework of a tangible destination, but rather within the tapestry of an eternal energy, where self-recognition is the only medium to feel and reach beyond that destination. And in the process of this journey, you will never feel bored or overburdened, but rather enjoy every moment, having realised the higher truth of eternity itself.

Here, liberation does not mean leaving this planet; rather, it means being fully aware of your existence in this mortal realm, enjoying every moment, seeing the blue herons and the chirping chipmunks, and finding your way here and there. You may feel that the destination around those valleys while you are stepping your tiny feet towards those mountains of your dream is the ideal destination, you wished for. Or you may have that same feeling while standing on a solitary beach, only to see that horizon where the sun meets the sea at every dawn.

You can also feel her presence even when you are surrounded by others, at your workplace or at a festive gathering. Whenever and wherever you go, she will always guide and shelter your being, bringing a higher state of consciousness within yourself. And I think this would be the only way to feel the presence of your eternal home. Throughout our entire lives, we are all searching for this, but we have never noticed it within. But there she is. If you feel her presence within your entity, every moment may appear before you as eternity itself. So, let's feel and enjoy every moment of your life. Here on this planet, every hour has a special significance; every moment is a special journey in itself. So you need not chase after a destination. She will automatically come around and say:

"Are you feeling lonely? Here I am with you and will be forever. Everywhere you tread, along the dusty roads, towards those Blue Mountains or along the ways where the stars are the only living creatures to talk with. I will be there for you. Feel Me, smell Me and live with Me, right from the deepest corner of your entity. Feel My presence during those hours when you feel that you are alive, feel My presence in the eternal truth of your Being."

Here, the 'Garden' is nothing but the garden of your own life (the experiences you are gaining from your life) that you need to nurture in that way, so that she can bring along that eternal peace and happiness within your being. Let us stay tuned to her song that is continually inspiring and guiding you to find your home, within. Just pay heed to her. She is still singing:

You are running to and fro
Perturbed a bit, which way to go?
The 'Destination' you need to meet
Which way, you are desperate to know,
Forgetting the truth, you are already with Me
To feel the eternity within!

24 | Surrender and Feel the Divine Within

Most of us have the idea that everything we achieve in our lives is nothing but the result of our own intellect and power. And quite obviously, we start to believe that we ourselves are enough to sustain in this world. And consequently, we never look back. We never ask ourselves where the source of this eternal energy that is continually guiding and protecting us to be whoever we wish to be in our lives comes from. We never question our positions; instead, we gradually start to incorporate ourselves into a framework of self-exaggeration —a conception of egoistic I-ness that sometimes ultimately leads us towards a state of doom and depression.

And at that very moment, we cannot find the true meaning of life itself, whereas, a few days earlier, we had already believed that it is only we, "ourselves," who have been the show-stoppers all through the journey of our lives. But is it really true? Is it really "we" who are responsible for all the success of our lives? Or is it something else, some cosmic power that is continually enlightening our existence in a divine way, helping us to believe in ourselves? And here, in this concluding chapter, I would like to take you along that path of enlightenment where truth resides, where you may have a correspondence with your true self, and, gradually, recognise who you are in reality and where the ultimate power of your being lies.

Depression: A State of Non-Recognition

Nowadays, most of us are quite familiar with the term 'depression', I think. But do we know what the term actually means? Some of us may think that it is nothing but only some sort of mental illness that sometimes may break into some unnatural, lunatic behaviour or sometimes may compel us to take any fatal decision. But this is only a superficial perspective that we know about depression that already has spread its wings, just like an epidemic in our modern, contemporary society, where everything has its own success parameter. And every time we prefer to see ourselves according to others' point of view, instead of looking at our reflection in a mirror, where we can only have a better image of ourselves. And I think this may be one of the causes of this depressive state of our society that has become more like an epidemic nowadays.

But for me, this depression is not like an ordinary mental illness that we often think of. Rather, it is that mental condition or that state of our being when we are spiritually alienated; alienated from that higher source of energy, alienated from the true recognition of our self. And do you really want to know where lies the cause itself? It is very simple, my dear! The actual cause of this, I think, during this stage of depression, most of the time, we forget about the higher source of intelligence that is governing the entire universe. Instead, we start to believe in our outer selves, in our outer conditions that have nothing to do with that inner seed we have within since the primordial time of our existence. And the moment we start to rely on those external circumstances, the conscious self of our mind quite automatically starts to take signals from the outer environment, and once again we become just like the puppets at the hands of that external situation.

On the other hand, our inner mind has another story to tell us. But we never pay any heed to that. Rather, we start to validate everything using that external yardstick. And the eventual consequence comes in the form of depression.

Though hackneyed it may sound, it has a deeper meaning. It is not only hopelessness that seems to pervade our existence throughout our lives, but also an alienated state of our being, where we do not even know that we are alienated; we are separated from our true selves. At that very moment, our conscious self is at its full play, and we are not even aware that we are gradually forgetting the eternal truth of our existence, which is far more distant from the megalomaniac, egoistic meaning of our life that we consciously feel as our only existence.

And as a result of it, depression spreads its power throughout our personality. We start to feel we are nothing but some hopeless creatures wandering here and there, with no meaning in our lives, with no worth to our existence at all. On an apparent level of understanding, it may seem to us that most of the time we confront in our lives is a consequence of failure. But actually, it is that spiritual alienation from which we are suffering, but are unable to recognise who we are and what our sole purpose on this earth is.

The Deeper Meaning of the Word 'Surrender'

Though on a superficial level of understanding, the word "surrender" means liberating yourself from all the bondage you have and devoting yourself to a higher authority whom you believe to have that special power to protect you. But if you probe deeper into it, you may perceive that it is not that kind of ordinary liberation that we mostly see, but a liberation from your egocentric self, from that I-ness which, throughout the time, compels you to collide with several forms of hopelessness, devastation, and failure.

And I think the moment you start to liberate yourself from that bondage or ego, quite automatically, you may start to believe in the highest force of intelligence. And herein lies the power of faith; the power of our being that most of the time we tend to blur by the egotistical tendencies of our behaviour. But there is a power of a divine light that is already within us. Though veiled on a superficial level, it is within the core of our soul since the primordial time of our existence.

Those of us who are ignorant of this fact always have a tendency to cling on that foolish ego and consequently suffer as a mere puppet in its hand, instead of transcending our consciousness towards that higher source of light and feeling our being in a divine way. As surrender to this higher source of intelligence is the greatest sign of wisdom, the greatest sign of the Truth itself. It cannot be defined in a theoretical way, but it has to be felt within the core of your heart. And in a deep silence, you can feel the magic of true surrender.

In this connection I would like to remind you of another fact that surrendering yourself to the divine does not mean to sit in a cross-legged manner, closing your eyes and continually demanding something good to happen, or forgetting all of your daily responsibilities and renaming it as one type of devotion towards God's grace. Because these kinds of things do not have any rationality at all.

On the contrary, it may beguile you to be a useless fellow who can only be considered as good for nothing in society. But a true surrender is a mutual correspondence between that higher source of divinity and your human self. And herein lies the actual meaning of true surrender, where we can transcend our consciousness towards that divine source of intelligence and, once again, may start to feel that we are actually not alienated from that source of energy; rather, we have that infinite power within our soul, within the core of our being. And herein lies the art of self-reliance, which is solely based on surrendering to that divine energy.

Death Is Nothing but the Death of Our Ego

The moment we hear the word "death", quite naturally, we tremble with fear. We start to think about what kind of devastation is going to happen to us. We start to think about our name and fame, about our family and belongings, about all our achievements, but have never been able to admit the fact that death is nothing but the inevitable truth of our existence.

We mourn for it; we ruminate over the loss. But do we ever know the actual meaning of this word "death"? Is it the real death that we experience, or is it a different journey towards that higher source of intelligence? Is it a different voyage that we all should experience someday? The answer is, "yes, it is". As our soul is immortal, she only changes her costume in every lifetime. Death in one lifetime is nothing but a change of the same journey that we are going through ages after ages, decades after decades. We are nothing but spiritual beings in human forms. Here we come on this earth in order to evaluate ourselves. We do our work according to our karmic destinations, according to our karmic needs. And with the help of those deeds, we mature and evaluate ourselves throughout this journey.

Our mortal body is nothing but a costume from which we generate our individuality and then, consequently, generate our ego. Gradually, we start to forget where we came from, begin to measure our importance by the yardstick of external circumstances, and identify ourselves with the ego we have. But we never tend to believe in that inner seed that we already have within the core of our being, the living source of our energy, our sustaining power. And that is why we start to consider death as the end of our life, while it is a gateway to a new dawn, a newer life of our soul.

A physical death cannot define the end of our being. A physical death cannot define where lies the exact meaning of the word "surrender", as it is not an ordinary process indeed. It is an experience that only some of us may have. And when it happens, quite automatically, you start to feel that you do not have any physical existence; you do not have any illness or botheration, but you have an existence that is somewhat transcendental. And at that very moment, you may only mumble a few words like:

"Thank you for what I have, thank you for what you gave to me..."

These were the written words that somehow, I managed to find on a tattered page of a diary that was kept by a bakery shop owner who once had been only an ordinary woman. But she never allowed herself to complain about her circumstances, rather always preferred to devote herself to her duties, her responsibilities and ultimately proved her worth through forming a bakery shop in her small town. You may be surprised to think where lies the extraordinariness of doing such ordinary work. Yes, you are right. There was never such fame to celebrate such work. But there had been devotion, a peace of mind that she got only when she found this breakthrough after a lot of devastating experiences in her life.

In the next section of this chapter, I am going to share with you exactly where she got that kind of energy to build her life once again in a newer frame of success.

Believe and Surrender to That Divine Light and Power

"Actually, I am satisfied with all I have now. You may think it as only a little bakery shop that does not have any value according to the yardstick of our so called socio-economic culture, but in spite of that, once again, I would say that it is nothing but a moment of satisfaction that I get every morning when I open the shop, only a few customers visit us, only a meagre amount of money that I can earn from this investment. But I never complained to anyone, not even to the higher authority of my office, who once fired me all of a sudden without any specific reason. I did not even complain to the landlord who once humiliated me, not even to God. On the contrary, I chose to be silent during the nights, and I started to maintain a diary of my own. That was not a simple diary to be written, but a diary of my release; may be a metaphor, to release all my thoughts. Gradually it became a habit for me...during the late hours at night I used to write and write without even knowing why I am doing all this...but I started to feel something better is going to happen...though during that moment life seemed to

me a dark dungeon from where escape was nothing but an impossible task to do in every facet of my life. And it was proved that I am a complete failure.

I had nothing to do, but gradually I started to feel that, at the end of that dark dungeon, I might find a light, and that light would not be an ordinary one. Still, the light that I needed the most at that very moment, the light of my own, the light from where I came and will be merged into, and this body to which I belong is just an outer shell of my real being that already surrendered to that divine light. You may ask me what special rank I got from that light. But my answer would be, I didn't get any special rank. Still, something special I got during that journey, and that special something was not momentary yet eternal to behold in my heart forever, and that was possible only through my complete surrender to that supreme intelligence. Gradually I perceived that actually I am not that much of a failure as I think of myself, rather a spiritual being living on this earth, totally surrendering my entity to that supreme power of the divine for a special purpose. And believe me, quite miraculously everything started to change all of a sudden, suddenly once again, I started to believe in that supreme energy and thought to rebuild my life in a simpler but graceful way."

You may wonder how it is possible for her to construct her life once again. Yes, this is really a radical question. But the answer would be like; it is only through a complete surrender that she has been able to lead her life once again. It is only through that complete surrender that she ultimately found her special something and felt that divine essence within herself. And it was only that divine essence within herself that made her thank God's grace and, moreover, helped her to believe in her life once again.

And herein lies the miracle of surrender, the miracle of transcendental consciousness that has the capability to enlighten us with the truth of divinity and make us believe that we are nothing but spiritual beings in human forms.